Yeah,
I Said It

Yeah,

I Said It

Wanda Sykes

ATRIA BOOKS

New York   London   Toronto   Sydney

ATRIA BOOKS

1230 Avenue of the Americas
New York, NY 10020

ISBN-13: 978-0-7434-8269-1
ISBN-10:   0-7434-8269-7
ISBN-13: 978-0-7434-8271-4 (Pbk)
ISBN-10:   0-7434-8271-9 (Pbk)

First Atria Books trade paperback edition September 2005

10   9   8   7   6   5   4   3   2   1

ATRIA BOOKS is a trademark of Simon & Schuster, Inc.

Manufactured in the United States of America

For information regarding special discounts for bulk purchases,
please contact Simon & Schuster Special Sales at 1-800-456-6798
or business@simonandschuster.com

I dedicate this book to Ava.
Welcome to the world, sweetheart.
I hope they don't blow it up.

Acknowledgments

Thank you to my family and friends for your love and support throughout my career.

Many, many big-ass thanks to Sara Washington. Because of you, I'm not on the phone with my business manager going, "What do you mean the book people want their check back?" Thank you for getting my thoughts and bits down on paper, and thank you for including your thoughts, too. I enjoyed working on this book with you although I know at times you were ready to toss me off the side of the Hollywood Hills. I'm proud of you. Good job.

Many thanks to Alyson Fouse and Dino Shorte. You always got my back. I truly appreciate your talent and friendship.

Much love to my partner, Lance Crouther. Thank you for holding it down at Brick to the Head Productions, Inc., while I was working on this damn book. You are a genius. I absolutely love working with you.

Thank you to Simon & Schuster and Atria Books for giving me this opportunity. My editor, Malaika Adero, thank you for not hounding me for pages and for trusting that I would eventually send you a book. You have been very supportive throughout this process.

Thank you to my team of agents at William Morris. Thank you, Mel Berger, you are wonderful. Thank you, Stacy Mark, a.k.a. "Agent House," for hooking up the tour.

Thank you to Jenny Delaney. I miss you.

Thank you to my publicist, Danica Smith, for everything.

Thank you to Mark Landesman and the ML Management crew. You make my life so much easier.

Thank you to the Miller & Pliakas LLP crew. Roger, have you ever seen a contract that you liked? You kick ass. Thank you for being my friend.

Thank you Riley for napping at my feet while I was writing and for chewing on them when you knew I needed a break.

Thank you to Tiffany Moss, I appreciate everything that you do for me. Don't quit.

Thank you to my manager, Tim Brewer. You work so hard to keep me focused and sometimes it actually pays off.

Thanks to the Comedy Cellar, the Improv, and all the other clubs that gave me stage time. And thank you to the fans for coming out to see me.

Most of all, thank you for buying this book.

Introduction
I Can Do That

You know, writing a book is one of the great American Dreams. It's right up there with finding your soul mate, or buying a home, or raising well-mannered, nonsociopathic kids. A book that will be read and adored and well received by everyone, even your worst enemies. But normally, most folks don't get the chance to do it until after they've acquired some sort of celebrity status. You see, when you're a hot commodity (and let's face it, right now, I'm on fire; did you see *Pooty Tang?*), you're supposed to write a book. I don't know why; it's just what you're supposed to do. One minute, you're sitting at home; then the phone rings. You answer it and it's . . . "they." The proverbial "they." They come to you and say, "Wanda, you're hot. You're it. Hot, hot, hot. WANDA, YOU NEED TO WRITE A BOOK!" And you get to thinking, Yeah. I *am* hot. Hey, a lot of people have done it. Why not me? I can write a "how I got to where I am" book, or a "what inspired me to greatness" book, or even a "whom shall I ridicule" book. This'll be easy.

People do it all the time. And not just actual authors, neither. Not just Stephen King, or John Grisham, or Octavia Butler, but other folks, too. Like running backs, serial killers, disciples, and hos. All you need is celebrity. Well, that I have, so I embarked upon the fun task of whipping out my book.

This is cool. I'll have my words and thoughts in print and they'll be forever recorded in history. More important, they offered me a check. And ain't nothing I like seeing in print more than "Pay to the order of Wanda Sykes." So, I agreed to do this; then I realized I was actually going to have to write this bitch.

I had a plethora of subjects to include in it. I mean, my mind was a fertile garden of humor just waiting to be harvested. And in that garden I've discovered one unshakeable truth: Fuck this! Writing a book is one of the most difficult things any human being could ever possibly undertake. I'd rather pass a kidney stone the size of a cell phone than have to do this again. That's a walk in the mall compared to writing a book.

What the fuck was I thinking? Hell, sometimes I can't even finish reading a book, and now I'm *writing* one? Oh Lord. I mean, hours and hours of just sitting at the computer, butt cheeks going numb, shoulders getting all cramped up from tension. Then I have to turn the damn thing on. My pupils literally shrinking from staring at the computer screen so damn much (I now use Times New

Roman font, 46 pitch), trying to come up with something good. Forget writer's block. I had writer's dam.

It's funny how you can just think up all kinds of hilariously funny shit while you're doing anything else other than sitting at your keyboard. Hell, I'm the Benjamin Franklin of comedy while I'm jogging, or out drinking, or swimming, or out drinking, or in the market buying drinks, or cooking dinner . . . and drinking. But man, when I got in front of that black hole called a computer, sometimes I was literally lost in space.

Do you know how many words it takes to even fill a decent-size book? Seventy to ninety thousand. Now if that doesn't sound like a lot to you, try it. It's not that easy. Sure, I could have just put down any old words, and several times during this experience you'll find that I did. But for the most part, I tried to make a little sense. The only thing is I get so distracted. Like right now. I'm writing this book and my mind starts to wander and all I can think about is, maybe I should ask my doctor about Singulair. So what if I don't have asthma? It wouldn't hurt to ask. I'll get back to this in a moment.

Well, I've got good news and bad news. My doctor said I do not need Singulair. That's the good news. The bad news is he also said if I ever call him at 12:45 at night again he's going to put my entire medical history on the Internet. That wouldn't be good. My mother never needs to know how hard I tried not to give her grandchildren. She thinks if I was going to be having sex, the least I could have done was make her a grandmother. Otherwise, I'm just a leg-spreading trollop. See, now that's got me thinking about grandmothers. Not the leg-spreading-trollop part, the other stuff. I should call my grandmothers. Wait . . . they're both dead. That would be a long-distance call. I'm sure somebody I know has a living grandmother that I could talk to. Hold on a minute. I've got to check this out.

Wow, you'd be surprised how many people have dead grandmothers. And once I brought them up, they forgot all about me waking them up on a work night. I heard so many stories about how Nana used to bake me cookies. Or that time Nana crocheted me a sweater. Even memories of Nana using her home remedies to nurse me back to health. Nana sounds like cheap slave labor to me, but three of my friends cried themselves back to sleep. Then that one wrong number I dialed started babbling something in Spanish and put a curse on my family. That should make it really interesting when we get together for Christmas.

Speaking of Christmas, you know it's never too early to get your shopping done. And since I'm already on the computer writing this book, I could go online for a little while and knock a couple of people off my list. Why don't you dog-ear this page and think fondly of your grandmother (living or dead), while I surf the Net. This shouldn't take too long.

Man, do you know how much shit is on that Internet? It's a virtual cornucopia. . . . Ooh, that's a big word. You think they'll count it as two? Where was I? Right, the Internet is a virtual cornucopia of bullshit. All I wanted to do is buy my nephews an early Christmas gift, but do you know how many dirty websites pop up when you put in a search for Xbox? I mean some dirty, filthy, nasty stuff. I think I saw my medical records on there. I went to over two hundred sites. I would have hit more of them, but my assistant started whining something about those pictures are gross, and if we're not going to work on the book, could she please go home and feed her cat.

Personally, I never liked cats, but if it would get her mind off actually writing this damn book, I was willing to ask her about the fur ball . . . bad move. Why the hell did I do that? She's more attached to that damn cat than most people were to their dead grandmothers. "Paws is so cute when he purrs . . . Paws won't eat tuna . . . Paws loves Michael Jackson." I wish Paws would choke on a hairball. I finally had to tell her to shut up. I'm trying to write a book here.

Besides, I'm a dog person and if you want to talk about cute, you should see the way my Riley chases his favorite ball around the house. He gets to barking and jumping around. Then his little tail wags so hard. . . . Hey, where's she going? She just walked out of the room. Was that my front door slamming? I think my assistant just quit. Oh well. One less person to nag me about writing this damn book.

Hell, I should be almost finished by now anyway. This piece alone should be what, thirty, forty thousand? Let's see what the computer says. Shit. This is only nine hundred and three words. I'm fucked. I wonder how much of the check they'll take back if I'm short eighty-nine thousand or so. I can't afford to do that. I've already invested most of that money. And I don't think you can return tequila. I'd better get serious about this.

Fuck it. I'm going to bed. I'll write some more in the morning. Well, not first thing in the morning, because I want to learn how to make a breakfast burrito. But I should be done with that by noon. Then I'll write. If there ain't a game or something on. If so, I can just pull an all-nighter. Shit, how many words is this now? One thousand and twenty-seven. Oh, they are so going to sue me.

Before You Start . . .

God gave us the ability to think. Being an American gives us the freedom to express our thoughts. I love my country. So please don't pull that Dixie Chicks scare tactic of labeling me "anti-American." Although in America you have the freedom to do so, just like I have the freedom to tell you to kiss my red, white, and blue ass.

Part One

Are We Mad?

I don't mean to disrespect the president . . . that's bullshit. You know I do. Hasn't anyone noticed that his eyes are getting closer and closer together? Pretty soon his left and right eye will be the same eye. If you look at him in just the right light (i.e., the light of truth), he resembles that weasel from the Kipling story, Riki-Tiki-Tavi. Talk about beady. And I'm supposed to trust this guy? He's either the greatest hypnotist since Svengali or we're just stupid.

Correct me if I'm wrong, but didn't we get rid of one president for lying about a government-sanctioned hotel break-in? And didn't we oust another because he lied about whom he had sex with? Last time I checked lying to us to justify a war trumps breaking into a hotel room and a blow job. Note the key word: lie. The only thing Bush II has done is get caught in lie after lie. Lies about the deficit, tax cuts, Social Security, the Iraq war. But we let him just keep on keeping on. What's wrong with us? Would we put up with that kind of treatment from anybody else in any other situation? Hell no!

Are we nuts? Why aren't we having a fit? Bush said that Saddam was an "imminent threat to our security." He said

Saddam had weapons of mass destruction. He lied. We didn't find shit. Then he tried to twist it by telling us they found some equipment that could possibly be used to make WMDs. What kind of bullshit is that? Either he's retarded or he thinks we're retarded. I took a physics class when I was in high school, that don't mean that I'm at home whipping up bombs.

Why aren't we in the streets screaming for him to be impeached? Are we under some fear spell? He lied. I've seen people more upset when Whitney is a no-show. Let Streisand cancel a performance. It's chaos. "Babs said she'd be here tonight. She lied! That cockeyed bitch lied!"

See, to me, America is like my car. I love my car. And my car is supposed to take me wherever I want to go as long as I keep the "governing" fluids changed and get regular tune-ups. That's what elections are: a nationwide tune-up—every four years. So that makes the president sort of like . . . our mechanic. And all we want from him is to just keep our shit running good. That's all. If he can do that *without* costing me an arm and a leg, cool. But, what if my mechanic was not only incompetent, but constantly lied about what's wrong with my car. A real-live Mr. Badwrench. Actually, more like a Mr. Fucked-up Wrench. Never fixed the car, just kept washing it. That's all, just washing it over and over and over again. My car's falling apart, but "it looks clean." Wouldn't I get a new mechanic? Or at least give another mechanic a shot? Wouldn't I report him to wherever bad mechanics get reported? Damn right. Look, in November, since we can't just up and buy a new car, can we at least get someone to get this bitch up and running?

Look Over Here!

We have U.S. soldiers being killed every day over in Iraq because of an unjustified war that Bush started. The economy is in the toilet. The education system is failing our kids. The deficit is out of control. However, instead of fixing any of this shit, the president focuses on nonproblems. We won't think about what is really going on if he makes us think that the real problems are steroids in sports, space travel, and gay marriage. You've got to be kidding me. Sometimes I feel like we're trapped on a bad Fox reality show, *Joe President*. He's not really a president. He's a construction worker. If he gets reelected, he gets a million dollars and we get screwed.

Enhancements

In what will hopefully be his last State of the Union Address, George W. said that we needed to crack down on the use of steroids in professional sports. When he said that, I was like, "Nigga, *what?*" I'm sorry, I rarely use that word, but he deserved it for saying some dumb shit like that. With all that's going wrong in this country, steroids in pro sports should not even be on his radar. Steroids are flying right above Nick and Jessica. Right now the president should *not* be concerned about athletes who are playing "too" good. The guy who has been unemployed for the past six months doesn't give a shit about millionaire ballplayers getting in trouble for using performance-enhancing drugs to elevate or in some cases sustain their careers. This broke guy isn't going, "Hey, I think there might be an outfielder position opening up in San Francisco. I better get my résumé together." This guy is wishing he could have taken some performance enhancers; maybe he could've kept his computer engineering job. Who is Bush trying to fool? Not me.

Now why shouldn't athletes be allowed to take performance-enhancing drugs? They get to wear performance-enhancing clothes, don't they? What the hell do you think a kneepad, or a bat, or cleats are for? To enhance performance. A football player isn't born wearing a face mask. But you'd think Jerry Rice was nuts if he went on the field without one, wouldn't you? I never saw Barry Sanders blast one up the middle without wearing a helmet. Or Ken Griffey Jr. slap a line drive down the third base line with his hand. So we shouldn't be upset if athletes take the "equipment" to the next level and make it "internal equipment."

How about shoes? Ever try driving the lane while barefoot? Don't shoes enhance normal human performance? Of course, but they're perfectly legal. So what if steroids can alter mental ability and capacity for clear thought? Talk about fun players, I'd love to see somebody get tackled during the National Anthem. There'd be bench-clearing brawls after the game. My kinda players.

So what if steroids eventually destroy the prostate and testicles and totally kill the sex drive? Hey, some of those guys need their sex drives tamed a bit. Holla at me, Denver! Hell, these guys need to take something with all that pressure they're under. It's not easy being a multibillion-dollar franchise player or even a benchwarmer. They've got so much to worry about: the games, the interviews, the parties, the checks, the chicks, endorsements, paternity suits, late-night car crashes, DUIs, murder investigations. No wonder they need some drugs to help them compete. Let them take all the steroids they want, if you ask me. Let 'em shoot up on the field, or snort during the half-time interview. Who cares? We just want a good game.

Space Program

Bush announced an initiative to spend twelve billion dollars to create a permanent moonbase by 2020. That's the first smart thing that he has proposed. He knows by the time he gets through, we will be so fucked on this planet that we're going to be needing another home real soon. We're not getting our deposit back on this one. We're going to have to sneak off and move in the middle of the night. Between the pollution, lowered emission standards, drilling, and pissing off every other country on the planet, Bush knows it's time for us to start packing up.

NASA, the JPL, it's the welfare for nerds. It is a billion-dollar welfare program for really smart dorks. Where else are they going to work? They're too smart to do anything else. They can't fit in with us. They know a bunch of stuff that us regular folks could give two shits about. They would annoy us to the point of hurting them. "Hey Wanda, did you know that the atmosphere on—" *Pow!* "Shut it up, dummy on the moon."

What have we learned from our space travels? Seriously? What have we learned or discovered that affects our daily lives? Nothing. We're spending billions of dollars in outer space for what? Why don't we spend just half of that to find out who shot Tupac?

I don't give a damn about space travel. I don't even have a passport, so you know I don't give a fuck about the weather on Mars. Shit, I'm not leaving the country, get caught up in a coup. Whenever they do discover something, the vast majority of us have no idea what it means. "Scientists discovered today that stars can be consumed by a black hole." What? Sounds like a report about Lil' Kim to me. "NASA discovered that an area of Mars was once drenched in water." And? Even the news anchor who reports the story don't know what the hell they're talking about. When it comes to that shit, they are just reading the TelePrompTer. Even Peter Jennings has that blank stare when it comes to that space shit.

Approximately twenty percent of Americans currently own a passport, so why are we dicking around in space? Ain't no happy Mars movies. *Star Trek* went there and shit went bad. I do believe that there is life on other planets. I also believe that we are the dumbest creatures in the universe. The Fox network is proof positive. I bet they don't dare have shows like *The Littlest Groom* or *The Swan* on Neptune.

I bet our Opportunity Rover is on the Martian news. "Those simple earthlings are at it again." To them, our rover is probably like the mosquitoes and the West Nile virus to us. "We're going to have to spray again."

Gay Marriages

It's spreading. The gays are going marriage crazy across the country. Massachusetts passed a law legalizing gay marriages. Also in San Francisco gay couples were lined up for miles because the mayor was issuing marriage licenses for same-sex couples. So now President Bush, under pressure from the conservatives, and needing any distraction to get our focus off the shit he's got us in, put his foot down and proposed a constitutional amendment to ban same-sex marriages. The president starts another attack, the war on the nuptials of Sam and Greg.

Bush said the amendment to define marriage as only between a man and a woman would "fully protect marriage." I don't think marriage needs to be protected from same-sex couples. The biggest threat to marriage is divorce. Divorce is kicking marriage's ass. Divorce is what ruined my marriage, not Stacy and Anna getting hitched. Most marriages end in divorce. If Bush and the Christian conservatives really want to protect marriage they should propose a constitutional amendment to ban divorce. Divorce is in direct opposition of their Christian beliefs more so than gay marriages. When you get married, and it's from the Bible, they say, "What has been joined by God let no man put asunder." See? Marriage should be like the Mafia—once you're in, you're in. Ban divorce. The murder rate would go up, but the institution of marriage would be strong and healthy. They're all just a bunch of hypocrites.

If you're not gay and you don't want to marry someone of the same sex, why do you care? Yet still in the twenty-first century people are trying to put a ban on things that don't even affect them. Remember those people who wanted to ban gangsta rap? They don't listen to the music, so why do they care? You never saw Tipper Gore riding in her Escalade sitting on spinning rims, with the seat set way back bumping to some Ice Cube. "Naw Al, I'm not feeling this new Cube." The same thing goes for the same-sex marriage law. If you're not a gender sleeping with the same gender, what makes this issue affect you to the point of making signs and marching to ban it? I'd only put that much effort into an issue if there were something in it for me. "What? They want to ban the sale of alcohol after ten o'clock? Where's my damn sign? I'm gonna go protest right after I sober up."

I'm so sick of these busybodies like Gary Bauer who are going around the country trying to ban gay marriages. Why do you care? Are you really losing sleep, tossing and turning at night in your bed because Bob and Jim are getting married? Why do you care, unless you were planning on fucking Bob or Jim? "That Jim is hot; now he's off the market." Somehow gay couples being married affects their straight marriage. What, are you afraid that gays are going to be more successful in their marriages? Your wife is going to throw it in your face. "Dave and Jake are so happy. They never argue." And you're thinking, Yeah, well, if you let me fuck you in the ass a couple of times maybe we'd communicate a little better, too. I'm sure that'll cheer things up around here.

The lame argument that they use is that marriage is a sacred union that is meant to be between only a man and a woman. By recognizing any other union, like a same-sex couple, it will desecrate the holy institution of marriage. I don't think the only prerequisite for a legal marriage should be that it has to be between a man and a woman. If you want to make marriage sacred, you need to be even more selective. Like, where the hell were Bauer and the protestors when Liza Minelli married David Guest? Y'all should've been out there trying to stop that shit, too.

It seems to me that the conservatives are hung up on the word "marriage." I say, let them keep marriage. It's just a word, terminology. Gays just want their union to be legally recognized across the country. What they really want are the same benefits that marriage offers, which in my opinion are none. So gay couples should just come up with a word other than marriage that means the same thing. Hell, come up with something that's better than marriage. Call it Mardi Gras! "I just got my invitation to Carol and Janet's Mardi Gras." Come on, who don't like a good Mardi Gras? You can't be mad about that. "Jake and Lester been Mardi Gras'd for thirty years." Don't let a word get in the way of your rights. Mardi Gras would be perfect. Gays love a good parade; have your Mardi Gras on a float. Give each other matching Mardi Gras beads. Write your own Mardi Gras vows. It will catch on. "Is this her first Mardi Gras?" "No, this is her second. She has three kids from a previous Mardi Gras."

A Mardi Gras would be wonderful. You don't have to subject your best friend to all that damn planning and inconvenience. No one has to worry about what to wear that day. Just come to party. You don't have to remember some unimportant words you spent the night before trying to memorize. Married couples would look at gays in complete jealousy. It's like married couples have to live up to the standards of what everyone thinks marriage should be.

Recently Married Person: Damn, I gotta go to the in-laws for Thanksgiving. I hate going over there. They're always pressuring me about how much money I make and about having children.

Recently Mardi Gras'd Person: Well, since our parents rejected us because we're gay, why don't we have Thanksgiving together with all of our other rejected friends? We can all get drunk and go out dancing until the early morning.

Recently Married Person: Damn, I wish I had a Mardi Gras.

He He He

The first time I saw George W., there was something about him that I didn't like right out of the gate. His laugh. The president shouldn't laugh like a villain. The man laughs like he just tied somebody to the railroad tracks. Now it all makes sense. Haliburton, tax cuts for the wealthy, his buddy Ken Lay skipping away from the Enron fiasco, the lies, losing millions of jobs, the war . . . he tied us to the tracks.

What's in the Cabinet?

We should've known the trouble that was ahead of us just from some of George W.'s cabinet appointments. It was like a bad joke. Let's start with the environment. Bush appointed Christine Todd Whitman head of the EPA. No wonder they've managed to lower the emissions standards. The governor of New Jersey is head of the Environmental Protection Agency. Do you know how dirty New Jersey is? I mean, I'm sorry, but you drive through New Jersey, you're gonna get a lump in your breast. Better get a mammogram at the toll. They should have a mammogram booth right next to the E-Z Pass lane. "That'll be two-forty, and put your titty on the counter."

I knew we were headed far to the right when Bush appointed John Ashcroft attorney general. The "compassionate conservative" went right out the window with Ashcroft. He just looks mean. Women and our right to choose were going to be challenged with Ashcroft around. When Bush appointed Ashcroft, I went out and got me four abortions. I stocked up. The doctor was like, "Listen, you're not pregnant." I said, "Hey, just shut up and do your job. I'm exercising my right while I can, dammit."

Condoleezza Rice, the national security advisor—I knew that was a problem right there. Come on now, you know a black woman can't keep no secrets. She was probably at the beauty parlor just tellin' all of our business. "I can't be in here all day. We're bombing Iraq at two. Just give me a press and curl. I want to look cute when we put our foot up Saddam's ass."

Approval Rating

During the early part of his term Bush enjoyed a seventy percent approval rating. The majority of us were satisfied with the job that the president was doing. Which makes sense to me, because he pretty much did everything I expected him to do. The economy is in the toilet. We're at war, and everything's on fire. He's met all my expectations. I have no complaints. He's right on target in my book.

We have such low expectations of our president. We let Bush get away with shit, lying and poor grammar. I think there are quite a few Americans who just feel like no matter what he does, we gotta get behind him. You don't pick on the slow kid. You don't do that. You don't boo at the Special Olympics. It's not nice. They're all winners. It's like when you don't say anything when the retarded kid eats his ice cream with a fork. You just let them enjoy their ice cream.

Didn't Get the Memo

It's been over two years and we're still waiting for the findings of the World Trade Center investigation. Who knew what? Could it have been prevented? What did he know? Basically, how did we fuck up? Everybody really wants to know: What did the president know before 9/11? Absolutely nothing. Remember, he didn't get smart until after 9/11. You can't hold him responsible for stuff that was going on back then. He wasn't paying attention during the briefings; he was probably busy coloring or something, unaware of the world around him: "Doo-doo-doo-doo-doo-doo-doo-doo-doo." "You want to listen up, Mr. President?" "Uh-uh, I'm busy, oh, go ahead. I want to finish this one. I think it might make the fridge. Hey look, Dick, I stayed in the lines this time."

We're not going to get to the truth because nobody wants to admit it when they screw up. Nobody, not the FBI, CIA, NSA, the White House, but they all screwed up. Instead of admitting it, they say, "Well, you know, there is no way in the world we could have imagined 9/11 happening. No way in the world. It was beyond our wildest imaginations." Then later on, here comes Coleen Rowley, the FBI whistle-blower, and we find out about all of these damn memos. Highly trained FBI agents were on it; they wrote memos like, "There are Middle Eastern men who have affiliations with radical fundamentalist Islamic groups and activities connected to Osama Bin Laden, taking flying lessons and they are skipping all of the classes on landing." You'd think that would've raised an eyebrow. Agents were damn near coming right out and saying, "I think this dude wants to fly a plane into the World Trade Center." But the higher-ups still said,

"Well, there's no way in the world we could have predicted 9/11." What? They are acting like the memos were written by Miss Cleo.

Cocky

When Operation Shock and Awe began over Iraq, George W. Bush was cocky. He couldn't start that war fast enough. When that statue of Saddam fell down in Baghdad, he was probably dancing around the Oval Office going, "Four more years, four more years!" He wasn't scared of shit. He landed a fighter jet on an aircraft carrier. He kissed Africans with AIDS. He didn't give a damn! "Bring those AIDS lips over here. Here's some money; go cure that shit." He let the real cowboy come out, wearing a ten-gallon hat, spurs, and six-shooters up in the United Nations, just acting a fool, guns blazing, "I don't need no stinking votes."

He's bombing everything. He's just waiting for North Korea to do something. He would love to get in their ass. He's just begging for it, like, "Please, please fuck up. I need another distraction from the economy." He's like black people in line just waiting for someone to cut in front of them. "Aw, please, do it, I wish you would."

The War

When you look at it, the war was pretty much written like a comic book. Our hero is out to avenge his father's defeat. That shit was personal. Saddam put a hit out on his dad when he was in office. I don't blame GW. If you mess with my dad, I'll whup your ass, too. However, I wouldn't lie to all of my cousins and friends to get them involved, too.

> *Me:* He tried to kill my daddy!
> *Cousin*: What? You should kick his ass.
> *Me:* Uh-huh . . . yeah . . . I should. . . . Uh . . . he said he was gonna try to kill your daddy, too.
> *Cousin*: What?! Let's fuck him up!
> *Me:* Okay. I got your back.

That's what Bush did. He was like, "Oh, you tried to kill my father? I will blow up your whole shit." Then he lied to us to get us on board. He told us that Saddam was going to kill us, and our daddies.

The whole war was playing out like a comic book. Our hero goes after the villain, they fight, our hero wins, but the villain gets away. Damn you, Saddam! Then there was the sequel, *The Search for Saddam*. As usual, the sequel stinks. We didn't get the bad guys. Bin Laden got away; we couldn't find Saddam. What pissed me off was when we couldn't find him they tried to appease us with a bunch of lovely parting gifts. The deck of Iraq's Most Wanted. What is that bullshit? Every day they were finding an eight of diamonds or a queen of hearts. That hand sucks! Do you really give a damn about the ten of clubs? "Oh look, we got the four of spades. That's Saddam's third-grade math teacher; isn't this wonderful? You can't be an evil dictator without knowing your fractions." "Hey everybody, the two of hearts, we found her. It's the shampoo girl. She's behind his hair. His hair is evil." I wanted the Joker. This deck is marked.

I was shocked when we found Saddam hiding in his filthy hole like a lil' bitch. When you know people are coming after you, you don't wait around for them. And we kept telling him, "We comin', we comin'." Why did he wait around? I mean, I missed three car payments one time. I knew the repo man was coming. Do you think I parked in my driveway? Hell no!! I hid my shit in a tree in Seattle. With that kinda warning Saddam should've been nowhere near Iraq. He should've been in some beachfront condo with a drink in hand, watching all the bombing on a wide-screen TV, like "Aw, damn, shit, not my palace!! I just put a new roof on that shit! Aw, he's fucking me up!! That Bush is crazy! Look at my shit! Run, Uday, run, Qusay! Aw, damn! I can't take it. Osama, roll that weed up, man. I can't watch this shit." Osama's firing up a fatty, saying, "Man, I told you not to fuck with Bush. Tried to warn your ass. Did you see what he did to my cave? Did you see my cave? Now the shit is just dirt."

It was personal. I believe Bush's former secretary of the treasury, Paul O'Neill, when he said that George W. wanted to go after Saddam as soon as he stepped foot in the White House. He probably didn't even unpack, he just started making plans to get Saddam. Richard Clarke, the former counterterrorism official, claims that Bush was so focused on invading Iraq that he didn't pay enough attention to Al Qaeda. He wanted Saddam. He was trying to figure out how he was going to get it by us. First it was:

Him: Saddam is in violation of UN sanctions.

Us: Let the UN work it out.

Him: Uh, Saddam kicked the inspectors out of Iraq.

Us: Well, because they were spying on him. Let the inspectors go back in.

Him: Uh, Saddam has weapons of mass destruction.

Us: Let the UN inspectors keep looking.

Him: Uh, we can't wait.

Us: Yes we can.

Him: He's an imminent threat!

Us: Prove it.

Him: Fuck y'all. We're going in.

We go to war; no, we attack Iraq. Can't find any weapons of mass destruction.

Him: Uh, Saddam is an evil dictator. We are liberating Iraq.

Us: Liberators? Where's the WMDs?

I would have respected Bush more if he would've just come right out and said, "All right, we gonna bomb Saddam because I just don't like his ass."

Whack-a-Mole

Is it just me, or did you notice it, too? When we found Saddam hiding in that little hole, he looked like he was not fazed by it all. I was checking out the footage of him being examined by the military doctor. Saddam looked as if he was more concerned about his health than the deep pile of shit he was in. He was rubbing his throat like, "Yeah, Doc, it's a little sore. I hope I'm not getting that flu that's going around."

Iraqi Freedom

I gotta be honest. I really could give two shits about Iraqi freedom. Has it changed your life? Is your hot water any warmer? When you wake up in the morning, do you feel the

Iraqi freedom? Does your food taste better now? It ain't free over there, especially for women. Women are still getting their ass kicked over there. I bet the day the Saddam statue came down a woman was out there celebrating her new Iraqi freedom, got caught up in the excitement, and hugged a man who wasn't related to her and she got shot in the head. "I'm free." *Bang!* "Aw, shit. I fucked up."

The way it looks to me, the Iraqis are free. Free to sweep up that blown-up country of theirs. Free to sleep under the stars at night.

You'd think with all this Iraqi freedom that we would get a little relief from the gas prices. I paid $2.40 for a gallon of gas yesterday. That's too high! And I drive an SUV 'cause I'm short; I like to sit up high. It's a big car. I burn up eight gallons just opening the door. I turn on the radio and burn up half a tank. I can actually hear my ride burp.

This environmentalist tells me I'm using up all our natural resources. "What about the economy? What about the environment?" Aw, shut up. I don't see you *walking* to your rallies. Piss me off and I'm gonna buy a Hummer.

I don't give a damn about Iraqi freedom. When gas drops down to twenty-four cents a gallon, then I'll celebrate right along with you.

Homeland Security

Homeland Security. They want us to feel safe. So how do they do that? By scarin' us to death. Every time we turn around, they tellin' us something is gonna happen, something is gonna happen. Can't even turn on the TV without hearing a warning, something is gonna happen. And they always do it on a Friday, 'round five o'clock. Just to mess up your weekend. You know, why don't they do it on Sunday night, tell everybody to take the day off Monday or something. "Uh—yeah. I ain't comin' in today. Naw, man. Something is gonna happen. Well, that's what Dick Cheney said."

Airports

I was wondering how long it was going to take them to put an end to the ticket agent asking us those security questions. What a waste of time, like if somebody were up to no good they were going to tell them.

Agent: Did you pack your own bags?
Passenger: Sure did, put the bomb in there myself.
Agent: Gate forty-five, have a good flight.

I don't think that the agents even listened to the response. I had this experience at the ticket counter. An agent asked me the security questions. "Did you pack your own bags?" I said, "Yes." "Have your bags been with you the whole time? You aware of all the contents of your bags?" I said, "Yes." And she goes, "Awesome." Awesome? What the hell is awesome? That doesn't make me feel safe. What, am I the only passenger who's been up here who knows what the hell is in their bags? Is everybody else who's flying going, "Uh—damn. You know, that's a good question because the dude with the FUCK THE U.S. T-shirt asked me to hold something. I feel like I'm going that way. I help a brother out, you know? I don't know what's up in here." "Gate forty-two B, have a good flight."

You, Over Here!

That random screening that they say they do at the airport? There's nothing random about the random screening at all. I know every time I fly, I get checked twice. They stop me at security, and then, they get me again at the gate. Once they actually made me go through the machine with the luggage. I'm like, "Man, this is ridiculous. This cannot be healthy, being all irradiated. What the hell is this?"

There is nothing random about it. You get to the gate, and they're standing there with a Sherman Williams paint chart. If your ass is darker than khaki, you gettin' searched. I've been searched so much I said the hell with luggage. I just put all my stuff on a hanger. "This is all I got, y'all. That's it."

War at Eight, Seven Central

Watching the war coverage out in L.A. was annoying. Those people have completely different concerns. "Who's doing the lighting? The lighting is horrible. The cinematographer should be fired." "The wardrobe is so blah. That must be right off the rack."

I support our troops. No matter what's going on or who's the commander in chief, I pull for our men and women who are in the armed services. I even pull for the Coast Guard. My dad, brother, and a few uncles were in the military. I grew up in that environment.

I'm happy my father is retired. If my dad were out there fighting in the Middle East we'd have some problems. I can see him out in the desert checking his pockets while his soldiers wait for direction. "Where's my keys? I know I put them around here somewhere. Anybody seen the keys to the tank?"

California Recall

My take on this is: You voted for the guy, you stick with him. You don't get a do-over. One hundred and thirty-five candidates, and it amazes me that some people actually got votes. If I were a California resident at the time, I would've voted for Gary Coleman. California has serious financial problems. Who knows more about being broke than Gary Coleman? He's qualified. But seriously, who would actually get in their car to go vote for Gary Coleman? Then again, I don't think you're driving a car if you're voting for Gary Coleman. You know you are taking the bus if you're voting for him. That or you're making a hiking trip to the polls. There should be trapdoors at the polls. Once you pull the lever for some bullshit, down you go. "I'm voting for the ex-porn staaaarrrrrrrrr!" Down ya go.

I can't believe Arnold won. Forget about the fact that he can't talk, never has been in office, he's an actor, groped a bunch of women, let's forget all about that. I thought it was over when it was alleged that he said there were some things that he admired about Hitler. I was like, "He's done." You just can't say anything good about Hitler. I don't care if you thought the man had nice shoes. You shouldn't say it. But what do I know? Arnold won. I can't wait to see the governor drive a Hummer to work on Earth Day.

Clinton

I was a big Clinton supporter, but I was so disappointed by him. I didn't realize the man was an idiot. The president was on national TV apologizing for getting oral sex. Why didn't he just stick with his lie? You gotta stick with your lie. You have to believe that lie wholeheartedly. It has to become the truth for you. The most powerful man in the world is on TV apologizing for receiving oral sex. He's an idiot. There are men I know who will gladly accept oral sex *on* national TV.

Why are you apologizing? Oral sex is not a high crime. It's not grounds for impeachment. Oral sex is not a misdemeanor. It's not treason. He got oral sex from a White House intern, not from an Iraqi secret agent. It was pretty patriotic if you ask me. He kept it in house. I like that.

If the man would've stayed with his lie he could have saved us all a lot of embarrassment. It's embarrassing. All the countries are still laughing at us. You know other world leaders were just prank calling him all day. All day calling the White House, "Hello, Bill? Guess what I am doing right now? Come on, guess. Would you like to speak with her? Oh no, she can't talk right now. Hey, now who's country sucks?"

They pulled out that blue dress and scared him. That little dress with the DNA, and he lost it. He gave up the lie. But my thing is, who's going to believe a woman who keeps a nasty dress? They oughta toss her right out of court. "Excuse me, Your Honor, she kept the dress." "What? No way. Case dismissed . . . and get your nasty ass out my courtroom! I should throw you in jail for being nasty, Miss Nasty Ass! What else you keep, some old Q-tips and some tissues? How old are those drawers you wearing, Miss Nasty Ass? Bailiff, wipe all this off where she was sitting, too." They pulled that dress out and he lost it. A little DNA. Bill's not smart. They had DNA, blood, a glove, two dead bodies, a limo driver, a barking dog, and O.J. still said, "I'm one hundred percent not guilty." Stick with the lie.

Boing!

I know I'm makin' more money, but where is it? I'm constantly looking at my portfolio, baffled. "Remember that check I put in here? Where is it? Is there a parasite in my account or something?" The economy is so screwed up. I had one stock that dropped to the point where I owed them money.

The country is in so much debt. That surplus we had is gone. We are deep in debt. Like trillions of dollars in debt, and we're still running up the bill. I'm fed up, so you know what? From now on, I ain't paying shit. I ain't paying one damn bill. I'm gonna be patriotic and behave like my government. When Amex calls me, I'll be on the phone chanting, "USA, USA." As soon as Uncle Sam pays his bill, I'll send my check in right along with him.

Martha Stewart

Why in the hell did they go after that woman? Martha Stewart. Insider trading? It's unfair. She's rich. Rich people, they talk to other rich people. And they talk about rich stuff, like stocks and bonds, and which island to buy.

They had it in for her. She didn't really do anything wrong. Everybody does that insider trading. Broke people do it, too, just on a different level. We all got a hookup. I have a cousin who works at Wal-Mart. She calls me all the time. "Girl, don't buy that today. It's going on sale tomorrow. Two for one, it's gonna split."

Basically, Martha is going to prison for talking to the feds. Well, so much for your cooperating with the authorities. What have we all learned? Don't say a thing without your lawyer present. I wouldn't give a damn if a sleeper cell was living next door to me; I wouldn't tell the government about it unless Johnnie Cochran was standing beside me. Martha really didn't do anything. Her kiss-ass big-mouth broker, Peter Bacanovic, is the one who called, alerting her that the Waksals were selling their stock. "Thanks for the tip. It saved me thousands and it might get me five years in the slammer."

The trial proved that it was a witch hunt. Prosecutors brought out testimony of Martha "yelling" at people on the phone, trying to make it seem that Martha wasn't a nice woman. What the hell does that have to do with the charges? They never would've asked questions like that if she were a man. Martha Stewart is a powerful woman; she probably does yell from time to time. She's the boss. Donald Trump yells at somebody every week on national television and fires him. We love it.

They scared Martha to death. I read in the *Enquirer* (so you know it's true) that she was having nightmares about going to prison, "lesbian nightmares." What is a Martha Stewart lesbian nightmare? "Shanice grabbed me by the collar of my prison-issued mandarin orange uniform. She lay down on the lower bunk, pulling me on top of her. She kissed me hard, then rolled on top of me. I felt the linen next to my skin, two hundred thread count! Aaahhhh!!!"

During tax season entire companies come out of hibernation just to teach the public how to lie to the government. But do we prosecute them? No. See, I think they went after Martha because they're pissed off about all the things she can make out of everyday items that they can't. I know Ann

Coulter or Rush Limbaugh wouldn't have a clue what to do with a skein of maple weaver's yarn. But should Martha be reviled and punished because she can make a quilt, a hammock, and truss a turkey out of that same skein? I think not. Maybe I'm just starting to identify with rich women more these days. I used to identify with poor women. Thank God money cured me of that sickness. Which reminds me, thanks for buying this book.

My advice to anybody thinking about committing a federal offense: Do it quickly. Get locked up in Martha's jail. You know it's going to be nice. Martha is going to spruce the place up. Also if you get bored, Martha can break you out of there. That woman can make anything. And it won't be any of that nasty, tunneling-your-way-out, ruining-your-clothes shit. Martha will have you walking out of there clean and neatly pressed.

It's Gotta Be the Suits

So let me get this straight. Martha Stewart goes on trial and is convicted for allegedly getting a stock tip from a friend and she made a few thousand dollars. Ken Lay, former Enron CEO, bankrupts a sixty-billion-dollar company and he hasn't seen the inside of a courtroom. It's gotta be the suit. You put a middle-aged white man in a suit and he can get away with anything. "He's not a criminal. Look at the suit."

Enron, Tyco, MCI WorldCom, just a few corporate scandals where rich guys got richer while the rest of the employees who were looking forward to retirement are now out looking for another job. These CEOs were just robbing everybody blind. That's why I got out of the market. After I saw my monthly report I called my broker, I was like, "Hey, man, put all my money in weed." The price of weed never goes down. That's a real blue chip right there.

What little punishment these crooks get is never enough. They just go to a nice federal prison. I want them to do some *Oz* time. They don't even get a real trial. They get a congressional hearing. And what usually happens is they plead the fifth, or they go, "I don't recall." And that's acceptable. They get away with it, that shouldn't be acceptable. You ask any woman, if your man comes home late and you ask him if he's been cheating on you, and he goes, "I don't recall." You're gonna whip his ass till he gets his memory back.

These CEOs, man, to be that ruthless, you're a scary dude. I tell ya, now I walk past a little gangbanger, I don't even flinch. But if I see a white dude with a *Wall Street Journal*, I haul ass. Before I walk by the Arthur Andersen building, I'm cuttin' through the projects. Cutting through the projects, you might just lose what you have on you that day. I ain't never been mugged of my future. No thug ever ran up on me, "Give me your 401K. Give it here. I want your college fund, your IRA. I want it all."

Part Two

Decency, Dammit!

Pollution, crime, poverty, disease, homelessness, war; these are just some of the things plaguing our beloved country. And yet, a Senate House committee has been convened just to talk about Janet Jackson's right jug. They say it's all about decency. Yeah, right. Coming from the country that virtually invented the dildo and the cock ring. But all of a sudden, these pork-bellied, right-winged hypocrites are up in arms "for the sake of the children." "It was such an indecent thing to do when so many children were watching the Super Bowl." Come on, how many children actually watch the damn Super Bowl? I know I didn't have any kids at my Super Bowl party. That's why it's called "party." And I've never been at a Super Bowl party where I had to ask a ten-year-old to pass me the bottle opener.

I just don't get it. Instead of wigging out over a nipple, we should be upset by the fact that she really can't sing. And how old were those songs? Come on—"Rhythm Nation," "Control," "Velvet Rope"? Shall I go on? Because I can. That's the real indecency. But a breast? Are you kidding?

And just who are the "men" complaining because they

saw a breast? Frankly, the dudes I was with were pissed off that she only showed one. What a rip-off. You don't tease a real man with one breast for two seconds. It makes them angry. Well, at least it was her right titty. That's usually your best titty. Remember, always fake left, go right. But now I've got to wonder whether or not she has a left. You know how rife that family is with surgery and alterations and such. Remember when Janet was a trifle tubby and wanted a smaller waistline, so she had some ribs removed? So I gotta wonder: Two breasts? More than two? Less? We may never know. I'm concerned.

Flashing her titty was an act of desperation. Janet had to do something. Janet was probably watching the show. During the National Anthem she was thinking, Beyoncé was amazing, and so classy. Then halftime rolled around, Damn, Nelly is on fire. I gotta follow that? I'm gonna have to show my titty. She was probably backstage shining it up. It was so ridiculous. When you stoop that low, you might as well just give it up. Now we know what's worse than being assed out.

I love how Justin Timberlake bailed on her after all the backlash started. Talking about he was appalled. You know damn well he was in on it. That's why he showed up. He was trying to get back at Britney for kissing Madonna at the MTV Awards. I must say, mission accomplished. He's like, "Britney, you got a kiss, I got a titty! Black, crazy Jackson titty, with jewelry on it!"

Kobe Bryant

I love watching Kobe. He's so energetic. The way he hustles up and down the courthouse steps, it's exciting! It was funny to me how people were "shocked" that Kobe was charged with rape. Why? All we know about Kobe is that he's real tall. His exceptional basketball skills say absolutely nothing about his character. I don't know how he's been able to focus on the court. He dropped forty points the other night against the Suns. I would be a mess, guilty or not. I'd miss a lay up, "Fuck you, I'm up for rape charges." I would be all in the stands, "I didn't do it. I swear I didn't do it."

Kobe has that silent confidence, but he's doing a few things that scream, "I'm scared like a mug!" But I think his biggest fear was facing his wife. He got a new tattoo on his arm and dedicated it to his wife. Slow down, Kobe; save some space for all those good prison tattoos. You know his wife is mad. He bought her a four-million-dollar yellow diamond ring. He bought her mother a big house. If I was his wife I'd be like, "Look, you better stop spending all my money. You might be going away for a while. I'm gonna have to put you on a budget."

Kobe Bryant, Mike Tyson, never would have thought that these two would've been charged with the same crime. Who knew what really happened in those hotel rooms? It comes down to who do you believe? My problem is that usually the woman was "up to no good" in the public's eye. "What was she doing in his hotel room that time of night? She knew what she was there for." Now I know there are women out there who are shady and looking to take these dummies for bad, but for the ones who just think it will be cool to hang out with a celebrity, poor judgment shouldn't justify rape. Just like if you were at a club at 2:00 A.M. partying your ass off and you get shot in the face, I'm not going to say, "What were you doing at a club that time of morning if you didn't want to get shot in the face? Everybody in there was wearing FUBU. P. Diddy was in there. Mm-hmm, you knew what you were there for. You get shot in the face, talking about, 'I just wanted to dance.'"

Or if you get knocked out while at an ATM, nobody is saying, "You know what you were asking for. You standing there, telling everybody, 'Hey, I got money, want some of this money? I got some good money.' You must've wanted to get knocked in the head. Mm-hmm, you knew what you were doing."

True, ladies, you should be allowed to drink as much as you want and get naked without being touched if you don't want to be. No means no . . . in a perfect world. But, we don't live in that world. Let's face it, men are physically stronger than us; you have to have some self-preservation. There are a lot of guys out there who seem to be nice guys, but when it comes to getting some free sex, these Dudley Do-Rights turn into Dickey Do-Wrongs. You will get screwed.

So my advice is don't put yourself in that situation. I know it sucks, but you gotta look out for yourself instead of hoping that the guys are going to have some self-control, because that's not happening.

A horny guy is like launching a nuclear weapon; there is no fail-safe on a hard dick. Once it's up, it's gotta hit something. There's no stopping it, unless you have some girl-friends looking out for you. They rush in like a Patriot missile and shoot him down.

That's why I wish our pussies were detachable. That way you could just leave it at home. There would be no confusion. Leaving it at home says, "I have no intentions of fucking you tonight. My pussy is safe at home. It's not even here in the building, because I know that I do not want to have sex with you." That would be so cool. Don't put it in your purse; leave it at home, because if you put it in your purse you'll be telling the cops, "And then he snatched my purse and stole my pussy. Yes sir, he snatched my pussy right out of my bag. Can I press charges for purse snatching, too?" And you know what the cop would say, "Mm-hmm, pussy in your purse. You knew what you were doing."

Mike Is at It Again

I was watching TV when the cops raided Michael Jackson's place. Breaking news, there were over seventy patrol cars headed to Michael's house. So many cop cars, I thought they got a tip that Bin Laden was hiding out at Neverland. I was like, "Damn, Mike, sleeping with kids is one thing, but hiding Bin Laden is too much. Man, you going to jail."

Well, no Bin Laden, it was just Michael being brought up on child molestation charges . . . again! Why are parents letting their kids hang out with Michael Jackson? That's what I want to know. I don't want to know about how Michael spends his money on gaudy, shitty art. I don't care about his mask-wearing, who-knows-where-they're-from kids. I don't even want to know how he breathes through that slit that he calls a nose. I just want to know why parents are allowing their kids to kick it with Michael Jackson.

On national TV, Mike said, "There is absolutely nothing wrong with sharing my bed with children." Wait a minute. He said, "Not only was it not wrong, but it was beautiful." Huh? "The kindest thing that you can do is to share your bed with a child." What the hell is that? Why are parents still sending their kids over to Mike's crib? You don't see Jermaine's or Tito's kids over at Neverland hanging out with dirty Uncle Michael.

I think the parents should be charged with child abuse right along with Michael. These parents are pimping their kids. "Go play with Michael, Mommy needs a new house." I don't want to hear this garbage about these kids have life-threatening diseases and Michael takes care of them. They're Make A Wish kids. Well, I guess their wish is "I want to be molested by Michael Jackson." Don't stand in the way of the little boy's dreams.

First of all, Michael Jackson is not a kid. Why are you setting up a play date for your child with a forty-five-year-old man? No parent in their right mind is going to let their kid go hang out with a grown-ass man. Michael Jackson? Shit, I wouldn't let my kid go hang out with Michael Jordan. And I love me some MJ.

These parents are just as guilty. You know damn well if Jake the forty-five-year-old cable guy showed up at your door to play with your kid you'd call the police. "There's a nasty-ass dead child molester lying on my porch."

Michael Jackson may not be a child molester, but he damn well has all of the trappings of a child molester. Pedophiles usually have toys and snacks to attract kids. Michael has a damn amusement park and a petting zoo. We aren't talking Chutes and Ladders and a bag of Doritos. Mike has roller coasters and a candy factory.

I don't blame the kids for wanting to hang with Michael. Kids love that weird shit. Mike wears funny clothes. His face is strange. He probably lets the kids play with his face like it's a Mr. Potato Head. Michael is the friendly monster to the kids. They love that shit. Kids love the Teletubbies. I know if a Teletubby popped up on my lawn, I'd beat it to death with a shovel. There'd be pieces of Teletubby all over the place. They freak me out.

I'm so sick of hearing that Michael was robbed of his childhood. He's a millionaire; ain't nobody robbed him. A little kid in the third grade who has to get up at 5:00 A.M., no food in the house so he's not having breakfast, has to dodge bullets walking through his project to get to the bus stop, take an hour ride to a decent school where he can learn something, now *he* is being robbed of his childhood.

Michael is just a crazy bastard. Robbed of his childhood, please! Mickey Rooney was in show business his entire life. You didn't see Mickey's grown ass sitting in trees, playing with monkeys, or having plastic surgery to be taller. Mickey didn't go get some extra legs put in. He didn't go, "I want Wilt Chamberlain's legs." No, his little ass grew up to be a normal, sane man.

Robbed of your childhood? You should make up for it now. Live your adult life to the fullest. Mike should be partying his ass off. You're rich. Buy some hookers, go to Vegas, gamble with the high rollers, drive race cars, shit, pick up a drug habit like all the other normal child stars.

I'm sick of people talking about, "That's why Michael hangs around kids, because he feels comfortable with them." That's bullshit. To a grown person, kids are boring. I can talk to kids only for so long before I'm ready to throw myself in front of a bus. "Oh God, where's the uptown express when ya need it?" Mike likes being around little boys because that is what he's attracted to.

You'll put up with anything that you want to fuck. Ever talk to a really dumb date and it made you want to punch them in the head? You're like, "Aw, Jeez, you're an idiot. Please shut your stupid mouth." But you don't say any of that, you just sit there and smile and nod, pretending to be enjoying yourself. Why, because you want to fuck 'em. I've been there. I'm just sitting there, thinking, Please don't say anything stupid in bed. I hope all of your smarts are in your dick.

Michael don't like hanging out with those kids for real. I bet as soon as the kid hits the driveway Mike is like (in a bass voice), "Jeez, he was so annoying." Mocking the kid: "But why? How come? Can I play with your nose?" Mike probably takes off those silly-ass clothes, puts on some boxers and a wife beater, pours himself a scotch, lights a Cuban cigar, and watches SportsCenter. "Damn kids."

Catholic Church

Michael Jackson hasn't molested as many boys as the Catholic Church. They are in trouble. I was disappointed, because I thought the pope was going to come out and just put his foot down. Just get in they ass. I thought the pope would just step out there and be like, "Look, you nasty bastards gotta cut this shit out, right now." And he should use those exact words. Because when you do something that wrong, the pope should be allowed to cuss you the fuck out. But instead, the pope didn't really say too much.

Then again, you know, pope is gettin' kind of old. Who we foolin'? The pope *is* old, y'all. It's time to start thinking about puttin' the pope in the Old Pope's Home. I'm sorry, the man can't even stand up straight. The pope is all doubled over. And then, they don't help by puttin' that big, old heavy hat on his head, and all those heavy robes and stuff. Lighten the man's load. Give him a little Burger King crown or something. Help the pope out. Instead of all those heavy robes, give him a pair of pajamas. Let him wear a little tank top and some shorts or something. That would be cool. Give him some house shoes or something. Help the man out.

And now the pope has a hunchback. I guess that's where he stores all the confessions that he hears from the priests. "Uh-huh, you did what? Oh Lord. Oh—oh, please, shut up.

Oh, oh. Oh, y'all are killing me. Oh, I can't hear no more. My hunch. Oh, oh. I hear them, the bells, the bells, the bells . . ."

They gotta get rid of that one-strike policy. If you get caught, we counsel you and send you off to another parish. What is that? All you're doing is telling the priests, "Okay, you can do it once, but that's it. Don't be a glutton about it." The policy should be, "We call the cops and they haul your ass off to jail." Treat them like the little child molesters that they are. Don't let them get away with that.

Your job shouldn't protect you from being prosecuted. The guy who works at McDonald's, if he molests a little kid, they ain't gonna ship him off to Wendy's. "Oh, you can't do Happy Meals no more. No, no. You don't know how to act around the Happy Meals. A little too damn happy. Gonna put you on the Frosties. See if that'll cool you off."

Transsexuals in Prison

Convicts are getting sex change operations while in prison, and guess who's paying for it? Yes, us taxpayers, unless you're reading this book in your cell. We are paying for it. Why? Because the courts decided that it was cruelty for these criminals to continue living in the body that they were born with. These felons are really women trapped in a man's body. Well, if that's the argument, I'm really a rich woman trapped in a poor woman's body. Give me Bill Gates's money. Actually, I'm really a six-foot, ten-inch NBA first-round draft pick ballplayer trapped in a five-foot-two body. Give me Jordan's jump shot and ball-handling skills. Put an end to my suffering.

I believe in rehabilitation, but obviously it's not working because they keep coming back. Now we're just making smarter, stronger criminals. Instead of giving them a weight room, give them yoga mats. I've never seen any threatening-looking dudes in yoga class. You can get damn near any degree you want in prison. That's cool, but shouldn't we reward folks who are law-abiding? If you're poor in this country, you're just ass out . . . especially if you're not a criminal. We damn near drive poor people to commit crimes.

Ed: Hey, Lou, did you get that job?

Lou: Naw, man, they said I need a degree.

Ed: Go to school.

Lou: Can't afford to, nobody will give me a loan.

Ed: My cousin is working on his law degree.

Lou: What school?

Ed: Rikers Island.

Lou: How'd he get in?

Ed: He shot two people.

Lou: I just want a computer science degree, maybe I'll just snatch a few purses.

Let criminals get fat and out of shape. Maybe then they'll be too lazy to commit more crimes and if they do . . . it'll be easier to find their big ass.

Stick It in Your Ear

The Supreme Court finally overturned the gay sex ban. Just think, somebody is being legally sodomized in Virginia right now. "Come on, Betty, it's legal; let's do it for the commonwealth." Why call it "gay sex"? Gay people aren't the only ones who can appreciate a little oral and anal sex. You know there're plenty of heterosexuals out there sticking it anywhere they can find an opening. "Damn, baby, you got some good belly button." Although personally, when it comes to the anal, "no thanks." I can't imagine that I would find any pleasure in that at all, period. One time I was in the hospital and they had to give me an enema before surgery. It was so painful just going in my ass. I don't want another enema. I told them the next time, just kick the shit out of me. That would be more enjoyable for me.

It was a ridiculous law in the first place. How you gonna tell people how to fuck? Adults should be able to have sex however they want . . . well, as long as it is with another adult. Some things I'm just not down with.

Having sex with animals should be illegal, mainly because it's just nasty. Although there are some guys out there who barely made it into the human pool. If you put a gun to my head and I had to choose between some freak and a German shepherd, I'd take the German . . . naw, I'd take the bullet. It's just nasty! Plus, it's cruel to the animal because we don't know if they are enjoying it or not.

Metro *What?*

I used to live in New York City. When I go back to visit, my girlfriends introduce me to their current boyfriends. They are what is known as "metrosexuals." Apparently, this is a man who likes to take care of himself, is well groomed, well dressed, and appreciates the finer things in life, but is not gay. Okay, if you say so. But, hey, he might not be gay now, but by the looks of them, most of these guys are just a swat on the butt away from turning. They're getting facials, manicures, pedicures, deep-tissue massages, they're in counseling, and they're taking yoga. Okay, so they're not gay; they're little bitches.

Why would you want a man who's more concerned with how he looks than he is with how you look? Yeah, some of them are very attractive, in a Prince sort of way. But if you were out on a date and some shit was about to jump off, who would you want defending your honor? Mr. Metrosexual, who doesn't want to muss his suit and has to remove his pinky ring before he can throw a punch, or the guy just itching to head butt the shit out of somebody, even in church.

I want to see the messosexual. The woman who just don't give a fuck. She wears flannel shirts, boxers, never combs or washes her hair, drinks beer out of the can, fingernails look like she's been playing in a dirty fan, but she loves dick. How many guys are going to be chasing after her ass?

Bunch of Thieves

I love music. It just helps you get things done. Any time you can bob your head during work hours, you realize you have a wonderful job. Nobody bobs his head on Wall Street. Whether it's working out on the treadmill, driving a car, or waking up in the morning, music will see you through. That's why I understand why people download music off the internet. I don't agree with it, but I understand. Downloading music is like playing a video game. You got a joystick. There is danger involved. To them, it's just another way of appreciating music. I look at it as a cheaper, criminal kind of way. And these people downloading music are the worst kind of thieves. They are too lazy to walk into a store, pick out what they want to listen to, and shove it under their shirt. They can steal thousands of dollars' worth of music without leaving the house. That's just disgusting.

I was not surprised when I heard that Tower Records was having financial problems. I think me and maybe six other people are the only dummies who are still getting music the old-fashioned way—we pay for it. Whenever I go into the record store, I see the same faces. It's almost sad; we feel like it's a losers' club meeting.

People download because nobody wants to buy or listen to a bunch of music that's not good enough to be released to the public. The majority of music artists have only a few good songs you wanna hear. That's it. No more. CDs include a few good songs and some wacky bullshit. There was one of those hidden tracks on a CD I bought. A dude played the guitar and hummed for sixty minutes straight. I went through all that trouble just to hear an artist hum? No wonder he hid this. It's shitty. Next time hide it on somebody else's CD. Bottom line, artists need to make better albums so people will want to buy them. Who wants to spend their hard-earned money on one hit and ten demos?

Artists get so upset about consumers stealing their music, but aren't most songs today made by taking other people's music? Let's face it; new songs are just old songs. I love hip-hop, but I find myself buying more rock. When I hear hip-hop, I don't think about buying it because I already have it. I'm in Tower going, "I really like this song. I'm gonna get— Wait a minute, that's Chaka Khan's 'Through the Fire.' I got that." Everybody gotta bite off somebody. Everything is either sampled or remade. Although artists pay some type of licensing fee to do this, they still make lots of money off of these hits. If music artists who sample are against down-loading, then they are just a bunch of greedy bastards. They are damn near extortionists. They want people to pay for what they stole.

Personalized Tags

I passed an '89 Ford Taurus that had personalized tags that read JESUS. Wouldn't you think He'd drive a better car? Didn't He suffer enough? P. Diddy shouldn't have a better ride than Jesus. Don't make the Lord look bad by putting His name on your shitty car. That's not good promotion for the Lord. Little kids see your raggedy-ass ride and think, Is that what Jesus gave you? Then they see 50 Cent getting out of a brand-new Escalade, sittin' on spinnin' chrome with a plate that says THUGG'D OUT. What you think those kids are gonna think? Hell, they'll probably be like, "I'm gonna rob somebody right after church."

Part Three

Don't Give Me Death

I wish I could be for the death penalty. I wish we had equality in this country so I could feel good about putting people in the chair. The problem is that the majority of people who get the chair are minorities, poor, and they committed a crime in Texas. Texas don't give a fuck. They execute somebody damn near every week. That chair stays hot. That chair is the hottest seat in town. It's like a U2 ticket. When the Super Bowl was in Houston, I was surprised they didn't fry somebody during the half-time show.

I'm against capital punishment because there is no equality. There are too many factors when it comes to who gets the death penalty. Race, wealth, lawyers withholding evidence, cops lying, witnesses being paid, and of course Johnnie Cochran.

After that O.J. trial I started a Johnnie Fund. I'm saving up, just in case I kill somebody. Whenever somebody gets on my nerves, I go check my Johnnie Fund: "Not yet . . . you lucky my show got canceled. You'd be dead right now."

Too many factors involved. It's not only who does the killing, but who did you kill is a big part of getting the chair.

Black man kills a black man, he gets the chair. Black man kills a black woman, he may get life because judges are sympathetic. They know how a black woman can drive you to murder with all our "attitude and sassiness." Thanks to quality shows like *Ricky Lake* and *Jerry Springer*, people probably believe that black women talk shit while they are being murdered. "Oh, I *know* you didn't stab me in my chest. You gon' pay me for this blouse, you stabbing muthafucka. And that's why you got a little dick. Go head, shoot me! You can't fuck no way." Black man kills a white woman, he gets the chair. Black man kills a white man, he gets the chair and then the gas chamber.

There is no equality. White man kills a white man, it all depends. White man kills a white woman, it all depends. White man kills a black woman, it all depends. White man kills a black man, he'll get a speeding ticket.

There should be a big crime board, like a menu. Everything is prix fixe. You killed somebody, you get life. Robbery, every ten grand you stole, gets you a year. It goes way up for armed robbery. Everybody gets the same punishment across the board. "Oh, you assaulted her, too? You get the combo time."

And it's been proven that the death penalty is not a deterrent. If you're a murderer, you're not thinking about how much time you're going to get. Those people waiting for their execution date aren't feeling any remorse. They're not thinking about all those people they killed and molested, they're just regretting that time in their life when they thought it was a good idea to move to Florida. They're thinking of all those crimes they didn't commit. People they should've killed along the way.

Murderer 1: Man, I knew I should have killed that motherfucker at McDonald's who always put cheese on my Big Mac. Now I'm gonna die a fat man.

Murderer 2: I should've stole that algebra test in tenth grade. Now I'm gonna die without a high school education. Damn, what type of job am I supposed to get without a high school education?

Murderer 3: Why did I stop smoking?

Green River Killer

If you are a convicted killer trying to escape the death penalty, you might wanna try withholding information. This murderer got life in prison without the possibility of parole for killing forty-eight women from 1982 to 1998. The police couldn't find most of the bodies so the district attorney cut a deal with him. He tells them where the bodies are in exchange for life in prison. The DA felt that this deal was good for the families of the victims so they could have closure. I don't think they should have made this deal. I feel for the families, honestly. However, I'm worried for future victims. You are rewarding this guy for being a good body hider. This is an incentive for future serial killers. Now they are going to get all creative in hiding the body to avoid the death penalty. "Under the bed?" "In a box of Cracker Jack?" "The woods?" "Fuck it, I'll just eat the damn thing. . . . Naw, I'm too sloppy. I'll have DNA all on my shirt."

Crime

I don't believe that blacks commit more crimes than white people. I know the jails may not reflect that, because there are more brothers in jail than white guys. However, jails are not a true representation of who commits crimes. Jails just represent who got caught.

I truly believe that white people commit just as many crimes, maybe even more than any other race, but they get away with it. True story, I was in the grocery store with my attractive white girlfriend. I had just picked her up from LAX. We stop at the grocery store, she grabs a bottle of water off the shelf, opens it, and drinks up. She was thirsty after her first-class flight from New York. I pick up a few things, get in line, pay for my items. She looks in her hand at the half-empty bottle (I'm a pessimist) of Gelson's Water and says, "Oh, I forgot about this. Did he charge you?" I say, "No." She thinks about it for a mere second, then says, "It's too much of a hassle explaining. It's only, what? Ninety-nine cents." And she walks out of the store. She passed several employees and a security guard. Not one of them looked at her thieving ass. Now I'm sweating, waiting for them to grab me. I haven't done a thing. I'm totally innocent, but I'm scared to death that they are going to charge me with influencing a good white woman to steal.

Now my friend "Sticky Fingers" was able to walk out with that water because nobody was looking for her to steal. She could have walked out of there with a side of beef, and I bet the bag boy would have helped her to the car.

When I go into a store, I don't even chew gum 'cause I'm scared they're gonna think I took it.

Manager: What's in your mouth?
Me: Bubble Yum.
Manager: We sell Bubble Yum. Officer!

Sometimes the store may not even sell what I have.

Me: Wait, I don't want to take my book in there.
Friend: It's the Gap.

Black people face discrimination across the board. Even black criminals are at a disadvantage because of racial profiling. Hell yeah, black people get caught more, because everybody is looking for us to fuck up. While you're pulling us over, following us, checking our twenty-dollar bills, white folks are getting away scot-free.

We all are guilty of profiling. If you see a white man running, you think, He must be late for a meeting or something. Hey, out of his way. When you see a black man running, you think, Who's he running from? What did he do? I'm calling the cops. Hey, somebody stop his black ass. This racial profiling has to stop. Quit following us, or you white criminals help us out. Team up with a black criminal. Let him be the decoy, while you're robbing them blind. I bet Dr. King would be proud.

White criminals commit the biggest crimes, too. A brother might rob a bank. A white man will rob a pension fund. The brother is going to get ten to fifteen years because he had a gun. The white guy will get a congressional hearing because he had a job and a nice suit.

A white executive can steal millions of dollars and never see the inside of a prison cell. A black man could never steal that much money. There are just not that many liquor stores in the country. I'm sure there are plenty of black criminals out there who would love to commit some white-collar crimes, but those jobs aren't available to them. That's why we need affirmative action. I would love to pick up a newspaper and on the front page read about a black CEO ripping off millions from his company, putting them in bankruptcy. I bet he'd be the first man to get the electric chair in a three-piece suit. They'll make him hold his briefcase and all. "According to your Palm Pilot (PDA), you have an electrocution scheduled in about fifteen minutes."

Guns

I was thinking about buying a gun. Then I saw Michael Moore's film/documentary *Bowling for Columbine*. Good Lord, there are too many fucking guns in this country. After seeing this documentary, I was like, "I'm *definitely* getting a gun." Apparently I'm the only one who's *not* packing. I need to protect myself from all of these gun-toting Americans.

I went shopping for a gun. The one I wanted was five hundred dollars. I started to buy it and then I thought about it. If I spend five hundred dollars for a gun, I'm shooting somebody. I'm not gonna let a five-hundred-dollar gun collect dust. I wouldn't buy a five-hundred-dollar coat and not wear it. Somebody is getting shot, flesh wound or something, then I checked my Johnnie Fund and gave it back to the salesman. "Not yet, not yet. Do you have layaway?"

Here's the deal, bottom line—the NRA believes that you have the constitutional right to own a gun. When I say you, I'm not talking about your black ass. I'm talking to white Christian men. Also white women. White women need to be able to fend off the crazy white-women-loving black men.

They think of it as us versus them. They believe that they are the law-abiding American citizens and the rest of us are criminals out to get them. They are waiting for the revolution. Because real redneck white boys know that they got an ass-whipping coming to them.

Now this is where we all should be patriots and embrace *our* rights as Americans. Yep, we should all join the NRA. If you want gun control, get Crips and Bloods, the Nation of Islam, the JDL, the Mexicans, Arab Americans, any minority group, and let's all go join the NRA. If all of us were card-carrying members who legally owned handguns it would scare the shit out of those boys. At the next meeting they would be like, "Look, Mohammed has a gun, José has a gun, Dante has a gun, Saul has a gun, Chang has a gun, and the *Queer Eye* guys have guns. We need some goddamn gun control around here. This is ridiculous."

So please join me, join the NRA. We would become a nation of whistles and noisemakers. You would get robbed by a dude armed with a flashlight. "He put it right in my eyes. I fell to the ground. I couldn't see a thing. I just gave him my wallet; then he high-beamed me and ran off."

Seriously, I don't need a gun. I'm easily annoyed. I would shoot people in my house that I invited over. In fact, I long for the day when we get rid of guns. But that's not going to happen. Not as long as we have poverty. They tried to get rid of guns, wait—they tried to get guns out of poor people's hands. Rich white boys are going to hold on to their guns. When Charlton Heston said "from my cold dead hands," he meant that shit. Although by the looks of him, he's starting to cool off.

The Toys for Guns program: You bring us a gun, we'll give you a toy. Ain't nobody using their gun to rob Toys "R" Us. How about a Jobs for Guns program? You bring us a gun, we'll give you a job. "Wow, Jamal, you have a Mac-10, an Uzi, semiautomatic shotgun, and a nine millimeter. Shit, that makes you CEO." "Henry, a forty-five, that's it? Grab a mop."

Part Four

Back to Africa

I'm not politically correct. I still say black. I say it because with African American, there's no bonus. It doesn't make your life any easier. You don't see black people standing around, saying, "Oh yeah, African American. Man, I'll tell ya, this beats the hell outta being black. We should've made the switch years ago. Oh, this is nice."

You don't see any of us going into Bank of America, "Excuse me, I'm here to pick up my loan."

"Uh, Ms. Sykes, you were rejected for that loan last week."

"Oh, that was last week. I was black then. See, I'm African American now. I'll just go in the vault and take what I need. I'll sign on my way out."

African American ain't helping nobody. You think Rodney King's black ass is sitting somewhere, saying, "Damn, if I just would have waited two years before I acted a fool, they wouldn't have been beating my black ass. I would have been African American." I understand that whole African American thing, though. Some black people want to get back in touch with their African roots, that's all. Then you have some black people who just don't give a damn. You tell them, "Hey, I just got back from the motherland." They're like, "Where'd you go, Detroit? Did you see the Temptations?" They don't care. I understand that attitude, too. I really do.

Think about it. Africa. I know we were taken from there. But not once did they try to come over here and take us back. I never read about any failed rescue missions. When Americans are taken hostage we go get them, right? We send planes, troops, bombs, Jesse Jackson. We go get them. Not once have I ever been out shopping and some brother just rolled up on me: "*Pssst, pssst*. Hey, sister, I've been looking for you for many years. Come, the boat is this way. We are going home!" Never happens.

At this time I don't have a desire to go visit Africa; hopefully it'll hit me to do it one of these days. I don't think I could handle that African heat. I would spend my whole time there under an elephant's ass trying to find some shade. Also when you go to Africa, you have to get a bunch of shots. And when you get back to the U.S., you gotta get more shots. That right there tells me to keep my black ass out of Africa.

Black Panther Woods

I remember when Tiger Woods was black. You don't know what he is now. Tiger was black when the sportswriters were covering him when he was an amateur. They were like, "Hey, this black kid coming out of Stanford is going to be the hottest thing in golf." As soon as he turned pro and won his first tournament, I read, "Biracial golfer wins first tournament." Oh, okay. He's fifty-fifty. He's fifty percent black and fifty percent Asian. All right, cool. Then after he won the Masters I'm flipping through *Sports Illustrated* and I read, "Tiger Woods is a quarter black." I'm like, "Damn, now he's down to twenty-five percent. What the hell is going on?" They're treating him like he's milk. You know, whole milk, half-and-half, two percent, one percent, skim. For every professional win he loses some blackness. Only thing keeping him black is every now and then his father shows up. "Hey, that's my boy. Don't try to steal him now." They're taking him away. One more major title and we'll read, "Tiger Woods has just been named the Grand Wizard of the Ku Klux Klan." Everybody wants you when you're a winner. But you know as soon as Tiger gets in trouble, what will we read? "Black golfer arrested. Black Panther Woods found guilty." The only place he'll be playing is on the public courses with O.J.

Eminem

He won an Oscar. Everybody likes his ass. He's a smart guy. He knows that no matter how accepted he is not to use the "N word" in his lyrics. White kids love his shit because his songs are the only ones they can rap along with word for word without getting the crap beaten out of them.

Black people like him because he's from Detroit. And if you've lived in Detroit as long as Eminem and escaped without gators and a fucked-up hairdo, you're cool, man. I think all his misogynistic and homophobic lyrics are just a front to make him appear to be something he is really not. I mean, how homophobic can you be if you look like a cute lesbian?

What the *#%?

I made a mistake one night and took a break while writing this book. I watched *The Apprentice* with Donald Trump because I like watching white people get fired on national television. Also I was waiting to see if the black people were going to snap when they got fired. I wanted to see one of them jump across that boardroom table and slap Donald's comb-over down his shoulder.

But lucky for viewers, we had Omarosa instead. I loved that show but the finale was disappointing. You mean to tell me Kwame can't get a job? Kwame, with an M.B.A. from Harvard Business School, is unemployable? What kind of message does that send? You know there was some black dude sitting at home watching TV saying, "*Kwame* can't get a job? I'm not getting shit with my G.E.D. Aw fuck this, I'm gonna go rob somebody."

Anyway, after *The Apprentice*, I turned to *Super Millionaire*. I'd been writing all day, I deserved a little Regis. A white guy, probably in his thirties, was on the hot seat. The five-thousand-dollar question was, "Dr. Martin Luther King Jr.'s I Have a Dream speech; what were the last three words?" His choices were:

A) God bless America
B) Liberty for all
C) We shall overcome
D) Free at last

I know you're thinking: That's easy. Well, you're thinking that if you're black. This white man was stumped. He had to use a lifeline for a five-thousand-dollar question. For those of you not familiar with *Super Millionaire*, the questions don't get difficult until you get in the fifty-thousand-dollar range. Even Regis looked at this man, like, "Come on, you dumb hick, it's February. You're making us look bad."

The guy, by the way, he was from Newark, Delaware, chose to "phone a friend." Regis asked him who would he like to call. This guy went blank; he didn't say it aloud, but you could hear him thinking, Shit, I don't have any black friends. It was ridiculous. Then he said that he would like to call his aunt. I guess he was thinking his aunt is old, she was around back during that time. Maybe she had a dog that attacked Dr. King, maybe bit him in the ass or something.

It gets better. The aunt gets on the phone; he reads her the question. I'm waiting for her to chastise him for calling her, wasting a lifeline on such an easy question. Wrong again, Auntie doesn't have a clue. Now Regis is physically getting annoyed; he's squirming in his chair, like, "Well, you can use your fifty-fifty and we will remove two of the incorrect answers." That's what Rege said, but I know he was thinking: Get this dumb-ass motherfucker out of here. He's embarrassing the white people.

He uses his fifty-fifty lifeline. Now he's left with:

B) Liberty for all, and
D) Free at last

He's scratching his head. You can hear Dr. King from his grave, going, "Free at last, cracker! Free at last!" The white boy must have heard him, too, because he got it right.

Do you see how fucked up things are? Do you see why there is so much discrimination? Do you understand why black people are so frustrated? I know this happened on something trivial like a game show, but to me it is a fine example of what we've been saying all along. White people don't know shit about us and they are not going to go out of their way to learn. I would argue that anyone not knowing the answer to such a simple question should be considered ignorant of American history. But that's the problem—since Dr. King was a black man, some white folks feel like that's black history. They don't have to learn about that shit, none of their concern.

Well, that's bullshit! It's also bullshit that we have Black History Month. Don't segregate us from American history, belittle our ancestors' contributions. White folks act like black history is a hobby or a special interest, like it's Greek mythology. This country was built on the backs of black people. We have just as much or even more of a right to this country than anybody. We are a part of American history, so know our shit. Learn the words to "One Nation Under a Groove."

No Energy

If you're white and wanna be my friend, please have some other black friends. I don't have the time or energy to be breaking mutherfuckers in. I just don't. You know who you are, too, asking all types of bullshit questions, like I'm a damn alien from another planet. If I hear any of the following questions or statements from any of my white friends, we're through:

> Can I touch your hair?
>
> Just got back from tanning. Can't you tell? I'm almost as dark as you!
>
> Don't you just love 50 Cent?
>
> Do you think you can teach me some of Beyoncé's moves?
>
> Will you please tell off my boss for me?
>
> Why do black people use the "N" word?
>
> What are your plans for Black History Month?
>
> Is your hair naturally curly?
>
> Why would you want to go to an all-black college?
>
> Was Malcolm X Muslim like "Osama Bin Laden" Muslim?

Just thought I'd spell it out for you in case you didn't know. If you've ever asked one of these questions to your only black friend, apologize immediately. After all, it's not your fault your parents raised you to be a dumb ass.

Boo!

George W. got booed at the Dr. Martin Luther King Jr. ceremony where the president laid a wreath at Dr. King's grave to honor his birthday. I'm surprised Dr. King didn't jump out of his grave and punch him. I guess Dr. King really is a man of peace. Why did Bush even bother? The war in Iraq, his opposition to affirmative action, failure of his promise to "leave no child behind," cutting back health care programs for the poor, denying certain groups their civil liberties, all go against everything Dr. King stood for. Bush rewrote the dream; "I see little black boys and black girls hand in hand with little white boys and white girls in uniforms, carrying guns, marching through the streets of Iraq to get the bastard."

I've heard pundits say, "How could they boo the president?" I watch a lot of FOX News, so I heard that quite often. Sean Hannity actually said, "Why would they boo? The president hired Colin Powell and Condoleezza Rice." Like that should make us all happy. Just because Bush hired two black people, we're suppose to think that he's cool with us. I disagree with his policies, so I wouldn't give a damn if he hired Oprah and Ali, I would still boo his ass. "Why would they boo?" That's just stupid. That's like saying, "I don't know why old people are upset with the president. He hired Dick Cheney." The geezers should be satisfied.

Black History Month

I try to avoid watching television during February because that's the time when networks dedicate a few thirty-second spots for a Black History Moment. The spots usually run during a show that has a black cast member. I don't think you'll catch one during an episode of *Everybody Loves Raymond*.

According to these spots, over the hundreds of years in this country, there have only been about ten black people who are of any historical significance. Every year it's the same group: Harriet Tubman, George Washington Carver, Louis Armstrong, the black guy who invented the stoplight, Jackie Robinson, Thurgood Marshall, Nat Turner (who is my favorite), W.E.B. DuBois, and Crispus Attucks.

Crispus Attucks, the first black man to catch a bullet in the ass during the Boston Massacre. Have you ever seen the lithograph *Boston Massacre* by W. Champney? Five towns-people were killed, but in the picture it looks like every British soldier had their gun aimed at Crispus. I bet he got shot more times than Amadou Diallo. Who trained the British troops? The NYPD?

My teachers were so proud about that stoplight. "Kids, a black man invented the stoplight." That's the one thing that all black folks know. I remember riding along in the car with my crazy cousin from Connecticut, and he would say, "You see that stoplight I just ran through? A black man invented that shit." Looking at the stoplight today, I don't think that we've really benefited from it as a race of people. Do you know how many black folks have been yanked out of their cars and beat to death while sitting at a stoplight? I know there are a lot of black men whose biggest fear is to be sitting at a stoplight and have a police car roll up next to them. "Damn! This stoplight is going to put my ass in jail. Fuck that black bastard who invented it." I know I've been running late on my way to an audition and I catch every red light, making me even later. I cuss that poor man out. "Look at this shit. If it wasn't for your inventive black ass, maybe as a people we could get to an interview on time and get a damn job. Fuck you and your stoplight. Why couldn't you have invented something helpful like an alarm clock? Asshole."

It's the same historical figures, but now they have to make the spots hip so it will be appealing to the younger generation. I saw a Black History Moment on the UPN that was hosted by the actor/comic Flex. Flex has a show on the UPN where he plays a single father raising his daughter. He's about fifteen years older than his little girl. Hey, he's doing the right thing; that's positive. Anyway, the spot starts with Flex saying, "You know the rapper 50 Cent?" How did 50's name get mentioned in a Black History Moment? He's not the first black rapper to get shot. Well, turns out that Frederick Douglass, the abolitionist, was the first African American who was honored on a coin. Guess what coin? Yes! A fifty-cent piece. We gotta stop that bullshit.

I want black history to be taught all year 'round as American history and let's do away with this Black History Month. It's really starting to stink. Because now, since we need some new faces, we are making just anybody a historical figure. Lester Jenkins, he's the first black man to win the Powerball. Lester won forty-three million dollars. Eight months and twelve Bentleys later, he was penniless. FUBU, "For Us by Us," the first black-owned clothing company to design a line of fur sweatsuits.

It's not like we would miss it. Nothing goes on during Black History Month, maybe an exhibit of black art, they rerun *Roots* and *The Color Purple*, and Popeye's will give you an extra biscuit with your two-piece. Maybe if there were Black History Month sales going on during February, it would add some excitement. I would love to walk past Foot Locker and see a Black History Month Blowout Sale going on. They got a sign in the window that reads ALL COLORED SHOES HALF OFF. I'm all over that.

Pass the Minority Baton

The U.S. Census Bureau reported that the Latino population is 38.8 million strong, making them the largest minority in the nation. It's true. I walked into Roscoe's Chicken and Waffles in L.A. and I thought I had walked into El Toritos. Nothing but Mexicans running this soul food joint. I actually sat down expecting them to serve me chips and salsa and a margarita for starters. It used to be nothing but old black people up in Roscoe's. Guess they died off and passed the minority baton to the Latinos. I ordered some chicken wings the other day and I listened to the waiter tell the cook my order in Spanish. I'm like, "Did I just hear the word 'burrito'? I ordered wings!"

White Man

I try not to, and for the most part I don't live my life thinking about what "the Man" is up to. What is the Man's next
plot to ruin me? Although black folks hear it a lot, especially
from family members. I remember as a kid hearing, "Yeah,
get good grades. The white man doesn't want you to do well
in school. He wants you to fuck up and be ignorant." "Make
sure you vote. The white man doesn't want you to have a
say." If there's an election going on, I'm voting. Now I vote
all the time just to piss him off. Hell, I voted fourteen times
for Ruben.

White folks were upset when Ruben beat Clay. It was like
O.J. all over again. "I don't understand, Clay sold way more
records than Ruben; he should be the American Idol." What
you don't get is that all you needed to vote was a phone.
Black folks love the telephone. That's the last thing that gets
cut off. Black people will be standing outside of their apartment with all their belongings on the street, talking on a cell
phone. "Girl, can I come stay with you?" And we have several phones in different names. If we could vote in an election by phone, Jesse Jackson would have been president a
long time ago.

But the white man ain't going to let that happen. I don't
buy into "the Man" thing. I don't think he has that much free

time. I think the Man has problems just like everybody else. His kids are getting on his nerves, his wife won't blow him, he hates his job, and he's trying to pay his mortgage before the Man takes his house. His biggest fear is he has to move next door to the other man. The black man.

Now I'm not going to totally discount "the Man is out to get me" mentality, because I understand where it comes from. Slavery. Here's where some white people will close the book and put it back on the shelf. "Fuck her, I didn't have anything to do with slavery. Get over it." Or a white person at home, "I'm so disappointed. Come on, Wanda, you're smarter than this." Well, to that I say, "Kiss my ass, cracker! You already bought it. I got your money." Before you throw this in the garbage, keep reading. "The Man" is a leftover from slave mentality. Slaves weren't allowed to learn or vote. The white man didn't want us to be intelligent or have a say in anything. So I understand where the mentality comes from, but it's old. It's like parachute pants. It's time to stop. I think the government should help.

I'm not for reparations. This is where some black people will put the book back on the shelf. "That bitch is crazy." Or a black person reading it at home, is going, "Fuck you! I want my reparations check. Shit, give me hers since she don't want it. I'm broke. Nigga, I had to steal this book."

I'm not for reparations, but I am for a college education for any black student. If you get in, it's paid for, full ride. If a kid knows he has a future, maybe he'll pay attention a little more in the first grade. I don't care what school he/she wants to go to, just learn something—Yale, Florida, cosmetology school, karate school, bartender's academy, stripper school. Just learn something! I don't care if it takes your dumb ass twelve years to graduate, just come out of there with a skill. Also, the government should help place them or have incentives when it comes to hiring those graduates. Yep. When a stripper graduates, the government should subsidize twenty-five percent of her lap dances for her first two years. By then, she'll have her pole work down.

Part Five

Average Joe

This is one of the few reality shows that I'll watch, *Average Joe*. This is the show where a beautiful woman unknowingly is set up with a bunch of average-looking guys. Well, actually some of them were downright ugly.

See, that's the thing about looks when it comes to men. Men can be fat, have bad acne, be hairy, unattractive, but still make it into the average pool. A woman can only be beautiful, average, or in need of an extreme makeover. An ugly woman is not taking a dip in the average pool. They'll drown her.

Anyway, the beautiful woman goes on dates with these average guys; then one by one she sends a loser packing and the last man standing is her true love. You know how these reality shows work, and if you don't, then I applaud you for having a life. There's always a twist. The twist with *Average Joe* is that after she gets all chummy-chummy with the schmos, they throw some "A men" in her face. Yep, they send in the good-looking guys to see if she'll fall for them and forget all about the average Joes. Of course, she does not. She ends up sending some of the pretty fellas home, too, with all of their emollients and hair care products.

Now this does not surprise me at all. Women have the capability of seeing past the appearance. That's how we all have dated an ugly guy. C'mon, admit it. There's that one guy out there that you knew he was funny looking when you met him, but you let him hang around as a friend. Then you kept spending time with him because he made you laugh. Your friendly outings started feeling like real dates. Next thing you know, you wake up one morning with this possum-looking bastard sleeping next to you.

And your friends know he's ugly, but they're not going to tell you. You can tell because when it comes to your funny-looking man, they say things like, "Rodney wears nice shoes." "He seems really smart." "He doesn't smack when he eats. That's sweet." They don't tell you because they've all dated ugly guys, too.

Now men, they don't have the capacity to get past the appearance. A guy has no qualms about telling his friend that his girl is ugly. Hell, he'll have the conversation with his friend and the girl could be standing right next to him: "Jay, what's up, man? What's up with this . . . this . . . this . . . ?"

They could never do *Average Jane*. There is no way a good-looking man would entertain a bunch of unattractive women period, let alone on national television. Say they did find this lone soul—if he hung around long enough, he would trample to death the average Janes as soon as the beautiful women showed up.

Gorgeous Monsters

It's common to see an ugly guy with a good-looking woman on his arm. However, you rarely see an ugly woman with a good-looking man on her arm. And if you do, I bet you she's in handcuffs and he's in a uniform taking her into custody.

Bottom line, women are judged by their looks. Can't get around it. Men are judged by what they do. That's why men can upgrade. An ugly man with a six-figure salary becomes "kinda cute" to most women.

Look at Donald Trump; he's no Brad Pitt. Check out the Donald's hair. He might as well just slap some dryer lint on top of his head. It would look better than that fucked-up comb-over he sports. It's awful. Donald Trump driving a bus, you wouldn't look twice at his ass. Donald Trump standing in front of all those casinos, beautiful hotels, and buildings with his name on them . . . "Who's that sexy bastard with the fucked-up comb-over? He's hot!"

There are no upgrades for the ugly woman. An ugly woman is just an ugly woman. I don't care what she does. An ugly woman could be a genius; she could cure cancer and somebody would still say, "Hey, did you hear about that ugly woman who cured cancer?" There would be jokes on late-night television shows: "Did you hear about the ugly scientist who cured cancer? Yeah, that's great. You know how she found the cure? Apparently, she just looked at the cancer and scared it away."

An ugly guy can do anything. He can even be a movie star, play any role. An ugly man can be the hero, the bad guy, even the love interest, and we buy it. The only role an ugly woman can play is an ugly woman. And they let you know it up front. "Okay, you're the unattractive friend, so just stand here while the rest of the cast talk about your ugly ass. And action!"

Look at the movie *Monster*, the movie about female serial killer Aileen Wuornos. Aileen was not an attractive woman at all. I guess all that killing takes up a girl's time from grooming and worrying about her looks. "Hmm, I need a facial, but I gotta chop off a head by three. That's my MO. I don't do any killing after three, gotta be back in time to catch *Oprah*."

Anyway, they cast Charlize Theron to play Aileen. Charlize did an amazing job. However, this is how Hollywood is so fucked-up when it comes to women. They wouldn't even let an ugly woman play an ugly woman. They would rather take a gorgeous woman like Charlize, make her gain nearly thirty pounds, spray-paint her face, give her some fucked-up teeth and a mullet, and call it a day. Just the thought of hiring an average-looking actor to star in a movie made them uncomfortable. They feel better knowing that there is a bombshell under all of that ugly makeup.

Hollywood ain't no equal opportunity employer. Do you

know how many average-looking actors were so fired up when they heard that they were doing the Aileen Wuornos story? This role screamed opportunity for all the ugly, overweight actresses trying to get their big break. They were probably holding up Aileen's picture to their headshot. "I look just like her, finally a role for me. It's my time! I got this gig in the bag." I bet you they were all lined up at the casting call, thinking, Shit, I'm gold. I'm the ugliest one here. In walks Charlize Theron and they're thinking, She must be lost. Look at those pretty teeth; she is definitely in the wrong audition. Then they read the headlines, "What! Charlize Theron? She looks nothing like Aileen. They'd rather waste four hours with her in a makeup chair when I can just walk on set camera ready? This is bullshit!"

Hollywood gets a kick when beautiful women play average-looking characters. They gave Charlize so much praise for enduring the extra hours of going through makeup and for gaining weight. It was like, "How brave of her to be seen on the big screen looking so horrific!" There's nothing brave about what she did, because she's *acting!* The person who needs a pat on the back is the woman who wakes up every morning of her life looking like what Hollywood would consider horrific. A little cold cream, Charlize is back to her gorgeous life. A little cold cream for the other woman, she's back to her horrific life with a shiny clean face.

When Halle Berry did *Monster's Ball,* people were like, "Wow, no makeup, no sexy wardrobe, she really stretched, very daring." She's still Halle Berry! Halle Berry is still a beautiful woman. It's like a doughnut. Sure, frosting, cream filling, and sprinkles would be delicious, but a plain doughnut is still tasty. Wardrobe and makeup, that's just sprinkles for Halle.

In *Monster's Ball*, a racist, played by Billy Bob Thornton, falls in love with a black woman, played by Halle Berry. Come on, who isn't going to fall for Halle Berry? Billy Graham would have tried to hit it. Even the Ku Klux Klan gave *Monster's Ball* four burning crosses.

Plastic Surgery

Ugly is going out of style. It's being eradicated. With all of these makeover shows, there's no excuse to be ugly anymore. Plastic surgery is in and so acceptable nowadays that if you're walking around looking fucked-up, people just assume it's by choice. "I guess that's how she wants her face."

I don't have a problem with corrective plastic surgery. If you got a fucked-up lip, you can fix it. However, this cosmetic shit is getting out of hand. Now the only way to tell if people are naturally ugly is to see how their baby turns out. Plastic surgery can make you look better, but it can't correct that cross-eyed gene that you're gonna pass on to your child. You better start asking to see baby pictures of his or her ass before you get married. If not, you're going to be looking at your baby, going, "Where did he get those big-ass ears from? He don't look like neither one of us." Yes he does. He looks just like your ass when you were in the seventh grade. Those ugly genes are getting passed on. Fuck the college fund, now you gotta put something away for your child's makeover fund.

I read that a couple in Florida got breast implants for their sixteen-year-old daughter. Everything fucked-up happens in Florida, must be from all that sun on the brain. Anyway, at first I was like, "This is ridiculous." This girl is obviously too young, and what kind of message are the parents giving her? "You ain't getting nowhere in this world without big titties."

After further thought, I'm like, "We haven't seen this girl; maybe she really needed a little help." Let's be honest, looks are important, especially for women. Who knows? Maybe breasts were cheaper than braces. Maybe her parents had a plan. They could've been like, "We'll spring for some titties and hopefully you'll meet a nice man and he'll fix your teeth."

USXXXL

Watching the news can be quite repetitive at times. I don't know how many times I've heard, "A new study says America is rapidly becoming increasingly overweight. Obesity is the leading cause for heart disease, diabetes, and strokes . . . blah, blah, blah." Just tell us like it is. This is a fat-ass country!

It figures. Every time you turn on the television there's a commercial for a new tasty artery-clogging treat for our greedy fat asses. Did they really need to put more cheese inside of the pizza crust? Isn't there enough cheese *on* the pizza itself? Who's the fat bastard who just didn't enjoy plain ol' pizza crust anymore? Who said, "You know what would make this crust taste better? If it was more pizza. I tell ya what, on my next pizza, just wrap another cheese pizza around it."

The crust is there for a reason. It's your warning to stop eating. It's saying, "Hey, this is it! After the crust, it's just crumbs. Get your fat ass away from the table."

It's sick the shit that they come up with. A double cheeseburger is already too much, but a double-double Quarter Pounder with cheese? C'mon, man. Why don't you just pull up to the drive-thru, stick your ass in the window, and just have them shove the burger right up your colon?

French fries just weren't fattening enough, right? So now

you can have them battered and then double fried. And you wonder why we have all these little fat-ass kids with bad knees and health problems and shit? It's the food. They aren't eating anything of nutritional value. Pretty soon the police will have to take over this obesity epidemic. "Drop those fries or I'll shoot! Put the plate on the ground, put your hands over your head, and slowly walk away!"

Vegetables don't stand a chance. If it grows out of the ground, we're going to dip it in batter, stuff it with cheese, or fry it up. We ain't happy until whatever that healthy thing was is now unrecognizable. "This looks like broccoli. Could you wrap some bacon around it, then fry it up? Oh, and let me have a bowl of ranch dressing for dipping." I know I'm going to have a lot of explaining to do when I get to the pearly gates, because when I see shit like this I be wishing all kinds of illnesses on folks. "Lord, just pluck him in his heart right now, Father. Let that ball of cheese get stuck in her throat, oh God. Just scare them, Jesus."

All that supersizing pissed me off. I used to eat fast food. I didn't have the best eating habits, but after seeing all of this excessive junk, I got grossed out. Don't get me wrong. I'll still fuck up some fried chicken, but now I only eat it maybe once a month. Actually, not even that often. And to be honest, I don't even miss it. All it takes for me is a commercial where you can "biggie size" or get the endless bowl of pasta, and I end up craving tofu. Yeah, that's right—tofu. I eat tofu. And guess what? I'm in the best shape that I've been in my entire life. I'm talking even from the womb. I'm in better shape now.

You know back in the days, for my generation, our mothers could get away with a lot of the prenatal "no-no's" of today. I bet just about anybody my age can look back in a family photo album and find a picture of your mother at least five months pregnant with you, belly all swole, at a party with a cigarette in one hand, a glass of bourbon in the other hand. We were born with bad habits. Today, there's no excuse.

I don't want to tell y'all how to eat, because I think most people are stupid so it would be a waste of time. Also, like I said, I'm not eating right all the time. However, I do think that these fast-food companies should take some responsibility for our fat-ass, unhealthy country and just be straight up. Let these big fat fucks know what they are actually eating.

Fast-food restaurants should be forced to change all names of food to their caloric composition. Instead of saying, "Yeah, I'll take the Big Mac, large fries, large Coke deal," we'll be forced to confront reality: "Yeah, I'll take the 'six hundred calories (thirty-three grams of fat) plus five hundred forty (twenty-six grams of fat) plus three hundred ten calories' value meal, please." "Would you like to supersize that? You get an extra one hundred seventy calories." "Sure, good looking out." Then again, I don't even think this would help because you know there's going to be some cheap-ass mug, going, "Naw, girl, get the number three value meal. You get five hundred more calories for the same ninety-nine cents."

Do It All Wrong

This country has no idea how to get in shape. We treat diets like it's a trend. "Hey, have you tried the fat-free diet? Hey, I'm on the Subway diet. Look at me, I'm on the water diet. Did you hear that Betty lost fifty-eight pounds on the cancer diet? Good for her, God rest her soul." Now it's the "low carb" diet. Everybody and their mother is on the low-carb diet, the Atkins Plan. He's dead. He fell on some ice evidently. He fell because he was probably light-headed from not eating enough carbs.

Maybe it's me, but aren't you on the low-carb diet if you just stop eating like a hog? Despite what the media and the food corporations say, carbohydrates are not your enemy. Beer companies now tout low-carb brewskis. Drink all you want, only twelve calories, and a DUI, but check it out, Your Honor—no carbs. McDonald's even has a low-carb menu. What's low carb at Micky D's? When the place is closed?

I don't remember all this carb crap when I was growing up. If you were a fat sow, it usually was because you ate like one. We used to call it a glandular problem: an overactive mouth gland. And what about a hundred years ago? Or even two hundred years ago? You think there were a lot of chubby slaves running around? No, because they exercised. Yeah, it was forced, but nevertheless, ain't nothing like a day of menial labor to burn off some vittles. Try it. Tote a barge, lift a bail in between banana splits. How about three thousand years ago? I've never seen a cave drawing of a fat-assed Neanderthal. Because having to track down, kill, skin, and cook your own food will definitely help shed some pounds. Listen, if you're going to eat like there's no tomorrow, then at least walk around today.

Bypass Them

Al Roker opened up a can of fat-ass worms. He really started something that is annoying the fuck out of me. I know I'm wrong for feeling like this, but I can't help it. Here goes: I'm sick of all of these obese people getting this gastric bypass surgery. It's cheating. Diet and exercise is how you lose weight. You're not supposed to lose weight by having surgery to shut off a large part of your stomach because you don't know when to say "enough." Stop being lazy.

To me, these cheaters really didn't accomplish anything, so I refuse to recognize their weight loss. When you see them, don't tell them they look good. Don't ask them how much they have lost. Ignore it. Don't let them get away with that bullshit, say shit like, "Did you do something different to your hair?" "Hey, you got new glasses." "Girl, you look so cute, are those new shoes?" Salespeople, if one of these sneaky bastards comes in your little boutique trying to find something for their new slender figure, look at her like she has some nerve bringing her wide ass in there. Don't bring her a size eight, tell her to go waddle down to Lane Bryant. We must stop them from cheating like this.

Fuck 'em, don't tell them they look good. There are people in the gym sweating, working hard, damn near about to stroke out trying to lose weight. Those are the people that I encourage. In a minute, I'll tell a 250-pound woman walking on the treadmill, holding on for dear life, "Girl, Beyoncé better not let Jay-Z anywhere near you." I'm not saying shit to Carnie Wilson. Surgery to physically make you stop eating, what kind of willpower is that? These celebrities are getting on my nerves. It's different if you're a poor overweight person who can't afford to live a healthy lifestyle. But the ones who annoy me are the people who have money. They have no excuse for not eating well. They can afford personal trainers, cooks; they could've found thirty minutes a day to exercise. They found two hours to eat. Instead of getting a life-threatening surgery to bypass your stomach, next time try bypassing the fridge.

Weight Loss

If we are gonna commit to losing weight, we gotta incorporate more physical activity and better eating patterns on a daily basis. So instead of getting gastro . . . try some of these methods.

METHODS WOMEN CAN USE TO GET IN SHAPE

Open your own doors.

Mow your own lawn.

Stop singing in a choir and go run.

Do your own hair. If you're getting a weave, you could potentially be getting a ten-hour workout on arms alone.

Rather than cry and be depressed over what your man didn't do for you, fight him.

TECHNIQUES MEN CAN USE TO LOSE WEIGHT

Wash your entire body when taking a shower.

Lick pussy while balancing on a stability ball.

Participate in as many ball games as you attend and watch on TV.

Do a jumping jack every time your girlfriend gets pissed at you.

Instead of driving home from work, push your car.

How to Raise Nonfat Kids

Throw away your child's plate when they're halfway finished.

Punishment for every extra pound gained will be to read a book.

Rather than giving your child a good spanking, stick your finger down their throat.

Slip them a twenty-dollar bill for lunch money, surely a bully will chase them around the playground a few times before they take their money.

Each time they lose a life while playing a videogame, make them run a lap around the house.

Personal Trainer

When I walk into a fitness club and see a personal trainer who is overweight, I head right for them. I feel better about myself; at least I don't know any better. I'm not going to pay for some skinny chick to be hollering at me. Give me the big, sloppy trainer. I can meet his expectations and goals.

He'll count the walk from equipment to equipment as part of my cardio workout. You don't have to worry about doing a bunch of long reps because all of that counting gets him winded. He knows the menu at the snack bar. "Girl, they got hot wings now." The overweight trainer builds your confidence and your waistline.

My favorite trainer was at this gym that had three levels. We would take the elevator. It would be the two of us, and the handicapped.

Voluntary Punishment

We wonder why America hates to exercise. It all began at an early age when gym teachers would punish us by giving us exercises.

Teacher: Sykes, you are ten minutes late to class. You owe me ten push-ups.

Ten push-ups!

The whole time I wouldn't be thinking about coming to class any earlier, I'd think . . .

1. Fuck these damn push-ups!
2. Fuck this class!

3. This is gonna make me sweat. Now I'm gonna be stinky for the rest of the day!
4. I'm not listening to his ass the rest of the semester!
5. *He* can't even do ten push-ups!
6. This hurts!
7. My arms are about to fall off!
8. Fuck this class!
9. I think I'm gonna puke!
10. I'm never doing push-ups for as long as I live!

What kind of sense does that make? We've been taught to associate physical activity with pain and punishment. That's why we don't wanna do it. Who wants to get up at 6:00 A.M. five days a week for a little pain and punishment? Nobody!

"Wanna go out for a few drinks tonight?"

"No, thanks. I gotta get up early for a little pain and punishment. I can't wait!"

Physical punishment is the reason that all the bad kids ended up being the strongest mutherfuckers in school. Some of our best athletes failed gym class . . . more than once.

Bad Kid: My strength has improved significantly since last year.

Reporter: Is Coach pushing you a little harder in order to win that district championship?

Bad Kid: Naw, I've just consistently been late to gym class every day this semester.

Those gym teachers would also give us a drill called "suicides" at the end of each class period. You had to sprint all the dimensions of a basketball court. Appropriately named "suicides," it was one of those drills that made you wanna take your own life. I mean, how do suicides encourage me to make physical activity an everyday part of my lifestyle? They don't! You don't see a suicides class scheduled between yoga and Pilates classes.

There's another way that we've been conditioned to hate to exercise. We don't see results quick enough. See, if we start drinking at 10:00 P.M., we want to be drunk by 11:00 P.M. If we smoke weed at 4:00 P.M., we expect to be high by 4:20 P.M. So we're like, "If I weigh a hundred fifty pounds at ten A.M., after an hour of exercise, I want to be one fifteen."

Part Six

I'm Gettin' Paid

March madness? Phooey! Who wants to watch a bunch of college players who aren't good enough to go straight to the pros? Let's face it, athletes peak at a younger age than they used to. What's wrong with going straight to the pros?

Maurice Clarett, for those of you who don't know, he's the running back who scored the winning touchdown in double overtime competition giving Ohio State their first national championship in thirty-four years. Coming off a season high like that, Clarett thought he was the shit, so he fought to go into the NFL draft. The NFL's policy states that drafting a player who has been out of high school less than three years violates NFL antitrust law and harms competition. The courts ruled in favor of Clarett, so now it's white girls galore for him.

Come on, don't you ever wonder what it is about the black athlete and the white girl? I'm shocked whenever I see a black pro player with a black woman. It's like, "Damn, he must really love her. How'd she do that?"

It's almost as if white girls get ushered in as soon as the brother makes the team. At the combines the coaches are like, "He just ran a four-point-two. Get him a white girl. Four-point-two? Blonde hair, blue eyed. Here's your jersey."

Back to Maurice, I don't think the NFL should have an age limit. It's football. He'll find out real quick if he can cut it in the pros. Football is speed, strength, reflex; it's not English Lit. When they call plays, it's just a bunch of numbers, colors, and lefts and rights. I don't give a damn if he's coming out of the fifth grade. If he weighs in at 260, got skills, and speed, let him play. Put the pads on; suit his ass up.

Why shouldn't Clarett be allowed to play if he's good enough to compete? Let the man get paid. He can always go back to school to get an education after his football career. I'm sure by then the facilities for the handicapped will be even better than today's.

It's football. It's not like he's Doogie Howser and skipping medical school. I wouldn't want some kid telling me I'm going to die. "Ummm, it's like, your liver is like, not so good. Actually, it's pretty gross. Dude, you're like, game over, man."

Some opponents say, "Well, he's not mature enough for the pro lifestyle." Bullshit! The Olsen twins seem to be turning out just fine. Football is a sport, but bottom line, it's entertainment. If Clarett gets drafted, he'll be experiencing some shit he would be going through if he stayed in school. Only difference now is that the money is going into his pocket instead of the school's endowment. And that's what the big stink is all about.

I don't fault these kids for going straight to the pros, Garnett, Kobe, LaBron. They're good enough to be in the pros, why dick around, risk an injury for a school who's making millions off of you? Big deal, they give you a scholarship. It's not like they are going to give you any free time to actually learn something. Check out the majors of these athletes at some of the big schools. Organizational leadership, sport and leisure, undeclared, liberal arts, therapeutic recreation, criminal justice. It's like getting a college GED.

Paid Pussies

Once these baby superstars hit the pros, it's on. Can you imagine playing against those big ol' guys whose paychecks suck compared to yours? And they've been in the league for years and years, watching young motherfuckers like you get all the attention. I'd try to disappear and fake all my injuries until I was as old as those other guys. Derrick Coleman caught on. Sports are the only place where you can get paid for being a coward.

> *Coach:* And, Sykes, you're up against Shaq tonight.
> *Me:* Think I pulled my hamstring, Coach.

It's not just in the pros. If you go to a college football game, you'll notice about twenty players dressed in regular street clothes on the sidelines or in the stands. These are the players who have paid for college by using red shirts and injuries. Most of them are just a bunch of ex–high school players too afraid to make that jump to the next level, but some dumb coach thought they were good enough.

They still receive all the social benefits of being considered an athlete. The only reason you see them out at parties all the time is that they don't have to be at practice in the morning. They're the guys at home sleeping with all the stars' girls when they're traveling to away games. They got the status of an athlete with the spare time of the unemployed. It's like they've pulled off this tremendous acting job or something. They got everybody fooled down to the coaches, athletic trainers, teammates, and fans. Even newspaper reporters will quote their comments for the sake of writing game summaries.

"What position do you play?"

"Injured."

Do you actually feel like you've accomplished something when you've sat on the bench all day? What do you say when you come home to your wife?

Wife: Honey, how was work?

Benchy: Aw, baby, they had these wooden chairs instead of the aluminum ones. My ass is sore.

Football

I used to think that football took place in this overbearing male-only environment that bled masculine domination. But the more I attend, the more I realize these football fans could actually be experiencing the straight man's gay pride parade. You see men painting each other's faces in bright colors. You see men proud to wear another man's last name on their shirt. You see some men wear no shirt at all. Think about the whole event. Hot wieners on every corner as you walk up to the main competition. Men open up the back of their trunk for a little tailgating. Ain't nothing like participating in a little preparty just to get you in the right frame of mind. Guys get so loaded during these games, you wonder what it is about this environment that makes men get drunk and holler another man's name out loud. If fantasy football isn't considered a gay activity, I don't know what is. Don't all men's fantasies contain sex?

Super Bowl

I've been to the last three Super Bowls. My liver still hasn't recovered from the one in New Orleans. I'm just waiting to pop up on one of those *Girls Gone Wild* videos; at least I hope it's Snoop Dogg's. I have one problem with the Super Bowl, not the game, not the host city, not even the half-time show. My problem is all the players who aren't in the game hanging around town. Why are they there? Your season ended a few weeks ago, shouldn't you be hibernating right about now? You and your team didn't make it to the Super Bowl, keep your ass at home, losers. Watch the game from your living room like the overwhelming majority of people do who aren't playing.

I was amazed at how many failures I saw this past Super Bowl in Houston. Man, were they gettin' on my nerves. No matter where I went, in the restaurants, hotels, parties, just big muthafuckas hanging out, hogging up space. These losers actually have the nerve to host parties. "Come party with Dante Culpepper?" Not after that season you just had. It shouldn't be any partying going on, you should be somewhere studying your playbook.

You'd think these guys would be too embarrassed to even show their face at the Super Bowl. Nope, they fly their family members out to the game. For what? So they can watch you watch the game from the stands? Do they not understand that they're losers? Why are they at the Super Bowl? It's not about you anymore. Yeah, your team was above five hundred this year. But that just wasn't good enough. I don't want to see you anymore. I don't care how much money you make, beat it! The Super Bowl is for the two best teams in the league. Shouldn't you be in the weight room working toward being the best you can be next season? Go run a tire drill or something.

I went to the NBA All-Star Game at the Staples Center this year. I didn't see Christian Laettner or Alan Houston there chillin'. You football players need to follow their example. And what do y'all say when you see one another?

Wassup, man?

It's good to see you here. Heard y'all broke five hundred this season. Congratulations!

Yeah, you comin' to my party?

You're supposed to be professional players; have some shame when you lose. Coaches should make it a rule. If I see any of you participating in this year's Super Bowl activities, you will be cut from the team.

Native American Mascots

A number of colleges and professional sports teams still have Native American mascots. This makes no sense to me. It's painful to watch, especially since I grew up a Washington Redskins fan. I don't want to see the headline "Cowboys Defeat Redskins." That just sounds wrong.

I would see Native Americans dressed in their traditional garb in front of RFK Stadium protesting the mascot. The problem is that a lot of people dressed up as Redskins, so the protestors just blended in as fans. People would ask them if they had tickets to sell. It was sad.

There are some individuals who are such diehard fans of their teams that they insist on keeping these names and images in order to preserve tradition. They are so attached to their mascots that they lack concern about who they are offending and how this has shaped America's perception of a people. I would be all for changing the Redskins' name. It is offensive. I think the worst one is the Cleveland Indians' Big Chief Wahoo. It's just a red face on a baseball, with a big toothy grin. It's the Sambo of all the other offensive mascots. I have never seen a Native American smile that hard before, not even at a casino opening.

Mascots are supposed to give good luck. If a dancing Seminole is considered good luck, why not require the team to stay at a reservation the night before a game. That'll make the wind blow in your favor. Native Americans have been some of the most unluckiest motherfuckers throughout American history. These people woke up one day and their whole country was stolen from them. What kinda luck is that? Pocahontas didn't bring John Smith good luck. Hanging around her almost got his ass killed.

You are jinxing your favorite team if you continue to support these ethnic mascots. If you really think it makes that much of a difference, consider using people who are assured good fortune. Why don't you use people who just won the lottery as mascots? They're lucky. I'll cheer for the "Washington O.J.s." With "the Juice's" luck, we'll be in the Super Bowl. Better yet, use Ryan Seacrest as a mascot. Week after week, the fans would be annoyed as fuck, but luck would be on your side.

I think the Native Americans need to try a different approach to protesting. Listen, you are being ignored. I think a couple of arrows on fire whizzing through a luxury box would raise an eyebrow, maybe open up a few ears. I'm just putting it out there.

Part Seven

Marriage Terms

Just look at some of the terms we give to this supposedly happy union:

Wedlock—Sounds like incarceration to me.

Marriage—Did you ever notice how the word "marriage" is one vocal inflection away from being "mirage"?

Jump the Broom—Something used to dispose of trash.

Tie the Knot—As in Gordian; almost as complex as marriage itself.

Ball and Chain—Speaks for itself.

Your Better Half—Which assumes that you're the fucked-up part of this union.

Even the terminology is trying to tell you something. You should listen. But most of you won't. And you'll screw up and do it.

Can Keep It

I've been married, and that sucks. A Mardi Gras sounds like fun. I'll never get married again. Yep, I said never. I think marriage is oppressive. I don't care how liberal your partner is, once you're married, you automatically assume man-and-wife roles. You go into the marriage thinking, We are equal; this is a partnership. As soon as you say "I do," you will discover that marriage is like a car. Yeah, both of you might be sitting in the front seat, but only one of you is driving. Most marriages are more like a motorcycle than a car. Somebody has to sit in the back, and you have to yell just to be heard. That's why I said, "To hell with that bullshit, I'll walk."

It's too many expectations. There are things that you are going to expect from him or her as a husband or wife. And there are things that will be expected from you as a husband or wife. For instance, if you two keep going out for dinner every night or he's bringing home takeout, somewhere in the back of his mind, he's thinking, Damn, when is this bitch going to cook a meal? He may never say it, but trust me, he's thinking it because he's been conditioned to believe that the wife is suppose to cook the meals and do all of that other bullshit, like clean, take care of the kids, and blow him on a regular basis.

Now for women, it really doesn't take all of that, because we really don't expect much from you guys. All you have to do, guys, is pay some bills and kill a few bugs. That's about it. You do anything above that, we brag to our girlfriends. "James vacuumed the living room. I didn't even have to ask him."

And guys, you have to pay your share of the bills. Well, you do if you want to drive the marriage car. You can be the stay-at-home dad and take care of the kids if ya want, but no matter how cool and appreciative your wife seems to be about it, in the back of her mind, she's thinking, Look at him, playing Mr. Mom like a lil' bitch. Shit, I can pay for daycare. When is his punk ass gonna go out and get a real job? She'll probably never say it, but trust me, she's thinking it. Check her out; you'll catch her just staring at you for a few seconds. That's when she's wishing you were somebody else.

The husband expects to be behind the wheel of the marriage car by default. It's just the way it is. Well, in my marriage, that's where I had a problem. I believe if you aren't pulling your weight then you don't get to drive. I was like, "Scoot your ass over to the passenger side. I'm the one who's putting gas in this mu'fucka." And as you know, two people can't drive a car at the same time, so that's how we crashed. We totaled our ride. Luckily, I was able to walk away from the crash and I have been happily hoofing it ever since. Walking is great exercise. It's stress free. I highly recommend it.

Check, Please

Who's footing the bill? That's who gets to drive. A friend of mine makes more money than her boyfriend and they are thinking about getting married. She asked me what I thought. I told her, "Don't do it." It didn't have anything to do with the financial situation; I just never tell anybody to get married. She insisted that I give her some real advice so I told her that they both have to be comfortable with the fact that she makes more money than he does. However, he can't be too comfortable with it. You don't want to come home and he's there in his drawers, lounging on the sofa, eating Fritos and rubbing his new gut, talking about, "How's my little breadwinner doing? *Ricki Lake* was real good today. Oh, I ordered a few things online today. Who knew Sean John made leather umbrellas? I'm sure you don't mind since you bring home the big bucks." She's still single.

Save the Date

To some women, marriage is really the wedding. Have you noticed that when a woman's ultimate goal is to get married, all she really thinks about is the dreamy, elaborate wedding? Not the aftermath.

> *Me:* Wow, you are actually getting married! Do you think you're ready?
>
> *Her:* Yeah, I've got all the bridesmaids' dresses picked out. The date is secured at our church. I'm gonna wear my hair down and long. All the invitations have gone out. I can't wait!
>
> *Me:* Cool. So do you think you're ready to get married?

Have you seen these women who don't even have boyfriends lined up, waiting to storm Filene's Basement or some other store for the big bridal sale? Hell, these desperate women will have the entire wedding planned before they even meet their future husbands. What kind of bullshit is that? You don't see single men saving up for weddings. We see single men blowing all of their money on strippers and beer.

Ask Him

Have you ever asked a married woman her opinion and you get her husband's opinion? And it could be about nothing or her.

Me: I think your hair would look nice short and curly. Do you think you'll ever cut it all off?

Wife: My husband likes my hair long and straight. He couldn't imagine the thought of me ever cutting it all off. There's no way he'd let me do that.

Me: You didn't answer the question. What do *you* think?

Wife: I think he'd think I'd look like a boy and that would really freak him out in bed.

Me: Hey, that outfit looks great on you. Where'd you get it?

Wife: My husband thinks it makes me look fat.

Me: Okay, the next time we talk, just put your husband on the phone, cut out the middle man.

It's like their personalities are on hiatus or something. All questions get forwarded to that stupid part of your brain that worships your husband. Please don't show your friends this side if you have it. If I offer you a compliment, don't ruin it with your husband's words. Take it. You need it. Trust me. Married friends, when your personality is taking this break, please don't answer my calls. I called to talk to you, not your husband.

The Vows

When you get married and have a traditional wedding, you have to stand there before everybody and God and say " . . . Till death do us part." That's the vow you make. Stay together forever. The divorce rate is sky high so basically everybody's just lying their asses off. I blame the vows. It's asking way too much of us. We don't know everything about this person. That's why we're marrying them. We don't know that he's going to clip his toenails in the living room.

Why don't we come clean? Why don't we just be honest? Instead of standing there saying "till death do us part" let's just go, "I'll give it a shot." Or "I'm cool as long as he don't do nothing stupid." Let's make the commitment a little more realistic.

They say marriage is a contract. No it's not. Contracts come with warranties. When something goes wrong, you can take it back to the manufacturer. When your husband starts acting up, you can't take him back to his mama's house. "Uh, he's broke. I don't know. He just stopped working. He's just laying around on the couch making a funny noise."

You can't do that. " . . . Till death do us part." See, that's from biblical times. Moses wrote that. That's in the Old Testament. That goes way, way back. See, they had no problems saying "till death do us part" back then because they didn't have that much long to live. They had great plagues during those days. As soon as that guy got on your nerves, here comes some locusts. The locusts show up and eat his ass right up for you, problem gone.

Now we got antibiotics, personal trainers, and tofu. We just hang around forever, getting on each other's nerves, waiting it out. One day you'll end up just looking at each other. "I see you got up today. You should start smoking."

Love Ain't . . .

Now before I start, let me just say that I read or more like I've read the Bible and I do believe in God and I've been baptized. So now let's get to the funny.

Ladies, if you really want to know how men think, read

the Bible. They wrote it. I know that the Bible is the inspired word of God, but He left it up to men to tell the story. I couldn't find a book in the Old or New Testaments that was penned by a woman. Even the books about women, Ruth and Esther, we don't know if they wrote their own stories; the authors are unknown. Ruth and Esther probably did write their books and then God gave them to a man to do a rewrite. "Mordecai, punch this up. And take out all of these hearts above the I's and those smiley faces. Jeez, this scented paper is giving me a headache."

"Yes, Lord."

"And who writes the Word in pink ink?"

You can tell men wrote the Bible, because it reads like an action movie. With snakes, floods, murder, an ocean voyage, a whore, and a hero. For men, all of that makes for some good reading.

It's no wonder they didn't let women write the Bible. If they had, it would have read more like *People*. John 11:35, "Jesus wept. He was wearing a flowing ecru robe gathered loosely at the waist and made-to-order open-toe sandals by Cobbler. The only accessory missing from this perfect desert ensemble was Mary Magdalene. Rumor has it that they broke up."

I've got to give men credit, though. They used the Bible to their advantage. I'm not just talking about the way they made excuses for the way they dealt with women. For example, Mary had to be made pregnant by God. Not some shepherd or even a wise man, but God. That's the only way a man would accept his wife having an affair. Hey, you can hold your ground if your baby's daddy is God.

What got me on this "men wrote the Bible" thinking was when I attended a wedding and the passage of Scripture of what is love was read. Listening to the words, "Love is patient; love is kind," it hit me that no woman wrote it. This was definitely written by men. They were trying to cover themselves, and God knew how they were going to be getting in all kinds of trouble and getting on our nerves. He tried to help them out with 1 Corinthians.

We've all heard them before. It's used a lot in wedding vows, and it's the perfect way for the minister to tell the bride, "Don't act a fool." Because he's reading it right out of the Bible.

Love is patient; love is kind.

Love is not envious or boastful or arrogant or rude.

It does not insist on its own way; it is not irritable or resentful;

It does not rejoice in wrongdoing, but rejoices in truth.

Love bears all things, believes all things, hopes all things, endures all things.

And now faith, hope, and love abide, and the greatest of these is love.

According to this, has anybody ever been in "love" for real? I know I haven't. Please, you couldn't find better fiction in Oprah's book club. It's obvious a man wrote this because he never actually said what he meant. But if you really want to know what's behind these words, let me translate them for you.

Love doesn't yell at him for hanging out with the boys all night. Love is just happy he didn't wreck the car or go home with one of the strippers.

Love doesn't want more than he can give you; it doesn't brag about making more money than him, or dare to think you're better than him; and if you are, don't tell him.

Love doesn't get pissed because he drank all the juice and left the empty carton in the fridge; it does not remind him about forgetting to pick up more, but praises him even though he's an inconsiderate jackass.

Love bears him cheating on you, believes it won't happen again, hopes he didn't get her pregnant, then endures his bastard kid.

And now if you can keep your mouth shut and put up with all his mess, he'll let you call it love, but it's really just convenient.

Now wouldn't you love to be at a wedding if they read this version?

Also you know the men who wrote the Bible were straight men, "Man should not sleep with another man." They didn't come right out and say women shouldn't sleep with women. They didn't want to rule out the whole three-some thing.

It's a Business

I'm happily divorced. I think marriage is an institution for raising children. That's about it. I don't see the other perks, myself. Unless you are sickly, then you might want to tie the knot. That's the only other reason to get married, have somebody take care of your sick ass. You know, somebody to wheel you around and wipe your mouth. But other than that, it's just for raising kids. This is what I believe. I think when you get married you're actually going into business together. You're starting a business, right? In all businesses, you have to have a product. Why are you in business? See, we were married seven years, no kids. So we went out of business. No inventory. Marriage is for raising kids. When you have kids, that's when you have to stop being selfish. That's key. It's no longer about you or me. It's just about us trying to raise the kids.

But when you don't have kids, you're just two grown people floating around in a house; after a while it's like, "Damn, you still here? Why don't you go home?" And plus, that marriage thing, I didn't get it. It didn't click with me. I was marriage illiterate. My philosophy was as follows: I was taking care of myself before I met you. You were taking care of yourself before you met me. Let's just continue down this same path. Let's be together separately. That was working for me.

However, he would come home and just say stuff to me that I just didn't understand. He would walk in the door:

Him: What's for dinner?
Me: What'd you cook?

He would actually say stuff like that. Sometimes I would say, "I ate already." As I was putting the scraps in the trash can. "It was pretty good, too."

He actually said this one time:

Him: I'm all out of clean underwear.
Me: Ooh, you need to wash. I did my laundry yesterday. I got a drawer full of clean panties. Look, you're welcome to borrow a pair of mine to tide you over if you like.

I just didn't get it.

A Divorce?

I think my parents are the exception. They've been together forever. When I got a divorce, they didn't want to hear it.

Mother: What? Oh, you're gonna get a divorce? It's just that easy. When things get rough, you just want to throw in the towel just like that? That's a bunch of bull. What's the problem?

Me: All we do is argue.

Mother: Let me tell you something, your father and I had a shoot-out. You hear me? He took one in the arm. Harry, show her where I shot you.

My dad pulled up his sleeve.

Dad: Went right through my bicep.

Mother: See, that's love right there. You gotta learn how to work these things out. He was wrong. I shot him. We move on.

It's So Hard

You know what's harder than being in a relationship? Getting out of one. When Neil Sedaka said "breaking up is hard to do," he wasn't lying. I know I won't get married again because breaking up is the hardest shit to do. It takes years to break up if you want to do it properly. If you want to be able to leave with all of your shit nicely packed in boxes and not thrown all across the front yard, it's going to take some time.

After talking with my divorced and single friends, we all have the same story, guys and girls. One day you wake up and look at your mate still sleeping and you think, I'm so fucking bored. I gotta get out of this shit. Your mate wakes up and asks if you're okay because you're biting your pillow with tears in your eyes. You just say, "I'm fine. I was watching you sleep." You know the relationship is over, but you know they don't know it's over. So now your dumb chickenshit ass has to hang around another year or two waiting for them to figure it out and break up with you.

There is an art to breaking up. We all have that friend who is living day to day, doesn't have a real address, they just "crash" at a friend's crib, and are always needing a ride. That friend does *not* know how to end a relationship. They say all the wrong shit, like, "I can't help it if I'm the only one who liked themselves before we met." Talk like that will get your car destroyed and a restraining order filed against you.

It's too hard to break up. I don't envy anyone who's going through one. It's like all the talking and the crying is just too much. Then you gotta act like you care as much as the other person does. You know when they're hurting you gotta act like you're hurting, too. "I'm gonna miss you." "Yeah, I'm gonna miss you, too." Knowing you're just heading for the door. You got to be careful not to pour the "I'm hurting, too" on too thick. One of my friends did that and his ass ended up in couple's therapy. Dragged the breakup out for another eight months, and cost him a couple of grand for the therapist. I told him to just pay the therapist to break them up. "This relationship is going nowhere, end it now. You two suck."

And then after the crying, there's that look. That sad, confused look on their face. That "Why? Why?" look. Oh, I can't take that shit. I can't take the pain in that look. That look is filled with disappointment and heartbreak and it's all directed right at you. That look will haunt you in your sleep. You can hear them, "You said you loved me." Then you start thinking, It would be easier for me to kill you then to have to go through this. It would be easier to shoot you in the head while you are sleeping than to go through this bullshit. At least if I shoot you, I won't have to look at that face. At least I'd get a different expression. A look of surprise or shock, like, "Hey, what's up with the gun, baby?" I can sleep at night with that look. I can live with myself with that surprised look as I'm walking out of the door.

At least if you kill 'em there will be some sympathy. People will comfort you during your time of mourning. That's better than having to answer a bunch of questions, like, "So, did they catch you cheating? Who's getting the house?" If you kill 'em, your friends will show up with a Bundt cake and some potato salad. "Sorry for your loss. We're here for you." "Thanks. Is that lemon frosting?"

That's why whenever there is a murder case, the first person that the police question is the spouse. The cops know who is the most likely person to have committed the crime. And if they find out that you were unhappy or were seeing somebody else on the side, you going straight to jail. They know that you couldn't break up and you took the easy way out.

Ask Scott Peterson about how hard it is to get out of a relationship. That's why he's on trial right now. I don't know if he killed his wife, Laci, but he sure looks guilty. He had the girlfriend on the side, talking about his wife knew about it and she was at peace with it. C'mon, man, there ain't a woman out there who's going to be "at peace" with her man cheating on her. And while she was pregnant, too! Yeah, she was "at peace," like the kind of peace they have in the Middle East.

Scott should have gone old school. Remember back in the day when men would just leave and walk out? They would be reading the paper, then just get up, "I'm going to get cigarettes." And then never come back. I understand that move. I totally get it. It makes sense to me. He was doing her a favor. He couldn't break up, just couldn't do it. He thought about it, probably tried to build himself up. "C'mon, man, you can do this. Just look her in the eye and tell her it's over. Yeah, yeah, I got this. Here goes." He gets up, looks at her, grabs his coat, "We need bread."

It's the End

Some of my girlfriends act as though life ends when they don't have a man. Men don't act like that. They act as though life begins as soon as the relationship ends. Late at the bar with some friends:

> *Her:* I wonder what he's doing right now.
> *Him:* I wonder who I'm gonna do tonight.
> *Her:* Nobody in this club even comes close to him.
> *Him:* Damn, she's got a nice ass.
> *Her:* Maybe he called my cell phone.
> *Him:* How about a lap dance?

Following a breakup, it's hard for a woman to move on. The only way she'll get through it is by spending time concentrating on herself, which is something our society tells women not to do. It's always, take care of the kids, put food on the table, and open up when I tell you. Men don't have a problem concentrating on themselves because more than likely they did that throughout the entire relationship. Selfish bastards.

My Next Damn Book

I'm going to call it *Hey, Just Stop Talking. Shut Up.* The entire book will consist of just one chapter, one section, and one page. On that page will be three enumerated items: 1) Shut Up; 2) Please Shut Up; and 3) Okay, I Get It, Now Really, Shut Up. It will be an analysis of relationships.

The five most feared words in a relationship are "Honey, we need to talk." Nobody wants to hear that sequence of words. My book will solve all that. It will teach you that if you're in a relationship and you want to talk, then just start talking. When you're finished, shut up.

I can speak from personal experience, as all great writers

can. It was once said to me, "Honey, do you think that we could set aside some time next week, maybe Tuesday, to get together, because honey, we need to talk." Tuesday? But today is Thursday. Now what kind of sadistic evil shit is this? You want me to wait almost a whole week just wondering what the hell you want to talk about? Meanwhile, I'm walking around on eggshells, watching what I say so as not to add more stuff to the stuff you already want to talk about! Grown people are really still children. And we all have vivid, wild, and ruthless imaginations. For most of us "We need to talk" translates into a host of other possible meanings: "Oh no, he's leaving me," "He cheated," "He found out I cheated." Please, don't do that to your partner. Don't make an appointment to talk, just start talking. And remember— when you're done . . . ? Yep, shut up!

Part Eight

They're Worth It...

People who have kids are the ones who pressure other people to have them, too. They don't want to be the only ones who blew it. They want you to share the misery that they are experiencing. Only a few will admit that they can't wait for the kid to get out of their house. Get married, go off to college, get locked up, they don't care, just get out.

The mantra of the majority of my friends who have kids is, "Kids . . . they are a lot of work, but they are worth it." However, I've noticed that whenever they say this, they never look you in the eye during the "but they are worth it" part. Usually they're looking down at the ground, past you, or up to the sky to ask God to forgive them for that lie they're telling. Watch 'em, they never look you in the eye.

They resent your childless freedom.

Parent: What're you doing tonight?

Me: I'm going out for dinner, then hitting a few bars.

Parent: Oh, you're going out? We used to go out . . . before the kids came. Ya know, you can come over and hang out with us tonight. I made fish sticks. Later on we'll probably play some Uno. Come on over, girl.

Don't invite me over under the pretense of having an adult night just to play with your kids. I don't want to spend time with your kids. The only reason you want me over is to distract your kids so you can have a moment of peace. While I'm coloring, or trying to show your dumb child how to connect LEGOs, or stopping them from eating Play-Doh, you get to watch a TV program that's not animated while sipping a glass of wine.

Why the hell would I want to go over to your house instead of going out? If I had said, "Oh, I'm gonna go dig around in the cans out back of the sushi joint to see what I can find," then yeah! Your fish sticks sound pretty good. If I had said, "Oh, I'm gonna go find a good Russian roulette game," then yeah! Uno would be loads of fun. Why would I wanna spend my night playing Uno with you and your kids? Your kid don't even know his colors. So instead of saying all of this, I just say, "Naw." Then the usual response: "Yeah, well you have fun. We gonna stay here with the kids. You know, kids . . . they are a lot of work, but they are worth it." I can feel them looking away even over the phone.

You can feel resentment. They hate that you're out there in the world running free. One friend got pissed that I was going on a little vacation.

Parent: Where are you going?

Me: Jamaica.

Parent: Jamaica. Are you celebrating something?

Me: Naw, just gotta few days free, so thought I'd get away.

Parent: Free days! Uh-huh. Ya know, we started to go to Jamaica, but Jimmy needed braces. Jimmy! Come over here, boy, smile and show Ms. Wanda, Jamaica. If you put your ear to his mouth you can hear the ocean. Kids . . . they are a lot of work (head to the sky, tears rolling down), but they are worth it.

I have nephews. They love spending time with me because I let them do whatever they want to do. They're not my kids. I don't care. Only thing I need to do is keep you alive. That's it. They come visit me. "Oh, you didn't want dinner? Okay, ice cream all day, how 'bout that?" I don't have to do a damn thing. Just scoop it out. "There you go. Eat up." I don't care about your diabetes. I don't care. I remember the first time they stayed with me my sister-in-law called me at midnight. "Did you have a hard time getting the boys to sleep?" I'm like, "Sleep? We sitting up drinking liquor, playing Nintendo." They're not my kids.

Kids

To me, it's hard being a kid these days. I wouldn't want to be a kid now. There's too much going on in the world today. They have access to too much information. Kids don't get to be kids. When we were kids, we were dumb. Our parents were dumb, but everybody was happy. I remember riding along in the car with my father as a little girl, looking out the window.

Me: Hey, Daddy, why is the moon following us?
Daddy: Oh, the moon usually follows little kids who need an ass-whipping.

It bugs me when people take their kids to places they have no business going to. The other day I was at a restaurant that had a bar attached to it. I was in the bar having a few drinks and this guy walks over to my section; guess he just had dinner with his kid. For whatever reason they both started heading to the bar. This little boy was running all over the bar, just knocking stuff over, playing in between the seats. It was really getting on my nerves.

Me: Hey, man, wanna get your little kid outta here?
Father: He has every right to be here.

Me: No he doesn't. This is a bar; we're all adults. You can't bring a kid in here. That's disrespectful. I don't go to the playground and drink.

Father: (pause) Good point.

Me: So take that little bastard outta here.

I'm not really a Lakers fan, but last season I got hooked up with these Lakers tickets. They were free courtside seats. I'm not gonna turn that down. So I was sitting at the game with one of my friends, just talking normal talk. And you know, every now and then I may curse. Well, as I reached over to receive my third margarita (there's bar service at courtside), I noticed this guy sitting next to me had a little boy with him. Instantly, I apologized for using my standard foul language. I felt so bad. I was like:

Me: Oh shit! My bad. I didn't see your kid there. I'll watch my mouth.

Father: Thank you.

Then about two minutes later I thought about it.

Me: Wait a minute. These are twenty-five-hundred-dollar seats. "What the fuck is his little ass doing sitting in a twenty-five-hundred-dollar seat? You better have a job to be sitting in seats like these. And you don't look like one of the Spy Kids. If you're gonna act like an adult, you're gonna hear some adult shit. Have you filed your taxes this year? How's your prostate?"

See, it's not that I don't like kids. Yeah, I don't like kids.

Now I ask myself, for real, am I gonna have kids or not? Nope. Plus, I've reached that age where you shouldn't have kids. You know, once you've passed a certain age you'll have an old-looking baby. You ever have a friend who had a baby too late in life and her baby is one of those old-looking babies? Like the baby may have been recycled. Or maybe that baby has been here before. It's one of them babies who look like they can drive themselves home from the hospital. You look at the baby and think, Didn't he march with Dr. King? He looks like Ralph Abernathy.

I'd have an old baby. That's what I would name it, too. "The ODB. The Old Dirty Baby."

Mommy Dearest

Ever since biblical times women have had this societal pressure to fulfill their purpose on earth . . . to procreate. But you'd think by now we would've figured out that some women just weren't made to have kids. Remember that lady in Texas who drowned her kids? It's too much pressure.

Being a mother is harder than being a surgeon. At least you get schooling and training first before they let you start cutting people open. Also you can quit being a surgeon when you're ready. Patients aren't going to keep following you around with a snotty nose: "Doc, Doc, Doc."

That woman in Texas homeschooled her children, which makes her look like a wonderful, giving mother. However, the reality is that she was trapped with them all day. You have to have the patience of Job to be a mom. Kids will make you snap! I know some of y'all are saying, "No, no. It wasn't because of the kids. That woman had emotional problems. She was sick." Uh-huh. Well, she didn't kill nobody before she had those kids. After childbirth she turned into a homicidal maniac.

I know having kids can make you snap because I know I got on my mother's last nerve. Thank God she didn't do anything crazy. Instead of hurting me, she would just play dead. I had this gift of gab at birth. The doctor smacked me in the mouth. So when my mother couldn't take it anymore, she would play dead to shut me up. Hey, I need a live audience.

Being a mom has to be the hardest job in the world. We're used to men running off being lousy or absent fathers, but a woman who leaves her kids is considered a monster. Have you ever noticed that when a man says, "Having kids is great," nine times outta ten, he says it when he's not at home with his kids? His kids are home with the mother, driving her nuts, so I guess it is "great" for his ass.

I was with a group of guys at a club on a late Saturday night. One of them was a soon-to-be father and the other dads were telling him how he's going to love fatherhood. "Being a father is the best thing." I'm thinking, Well, I guess it is. You're here. You're going on with your life, sipping on beer and eating chicken wings while your wife is at home trying to figure out which child to throw out the window first. The next time I hear a man say some bullshit like that I would love for his baby's mama to magically appear and just slap the shit out of him, then leave the kids with him and disappear. Enjoy!

Adoption

People always ask, "Well, don't you really regret not having kids?" And I go, "Not really." Then if they keep asking, I always say, "Well, you know, maybe one day I'll adopt." But I don't mean that. I don't. It's just something I say to make me sound like a nicer person, that's all. I don't mean that bullshit. Don't I sound sweet when I say that?

I know I shouldn't adopt. I'm the type of person who will

buy a pair of shoes, wear them for a month, and find out that they don't fit right. They rub against my anklebone. It's irritating, so I take them back to the store. Well, I don't see why I would change my approach when it comes to any other purchase. I don't want to get a kid; then after two years I'm standing in front of the orphanage, going, "Sorry, lil' fella, it's not your fault. It's me. I have sensitive ankles. I need to see other kids." That would send me straight to hell. It would be nice to help some poor unfortunate kid, but I'm trying to save my soul.

It's hard for white couples to adopt white babies. The supply is low. That's why you see white couples with Chinese or biracial babies. Some black groups are putting up a fight to make it harder for white couples to adopt black babies. Me, I don't care. I'm not going to do it, so if there's a nice white couple out there who wants to give a black kid a good home, I wish them all the best.

However, I'm going to be a little suspect if these white folks start adopting the strongest and fastest kids. I don't want to see them down at the orphanage with a stopwatch holding trials, like it's the NFL draft. "Honey, let's get that one, look at his time." They get the kid home, he starts playing on the computer, white dad is like, "Leave that alone, son, let's go work on your crossover dribble." This is the kinda shit we gotta stay on top of. Twenty years from now I don't want to be at the Lakers game and the starting forward is Kwame Silverstein.

Elizabeth Smart

They found Elizabeth Smart. That was a beautiful and amazing story. My heart goes out to the family. That's a strong family. They never gave up hope. They waited nine months and stuck in there. Maybe that's why I don't have kids, because after three months they would've called me and said:

> *Police:* Ms. Sykes, we found your daughter.
> *Me:* My who?
> *Police:* Your daughter. We actually found her two weeks ago, but it took us a while to track you down.
> *Me:* Yeah, I moved.

She would've walked into her room—or my new billiard lounge—and I'd explain, "Well, you know how playing pool calms Mama down, so rack 'em up and we'll catch up on old times."

Elizabeth said she was surprised that while she was gone her brother got straight As in school. I thought that was kinda messed up, too. She was like, "So you were just able to hit the books, huh? Nothing on your mind? Nothing bothering you? You were just able to focus and concentrate on your studies? I guess the lighting was better in my room."

I was hoping they would go quietly back to having a normal life. Then all the TV interviews and magazine stories started rolling out. What kind of parents get rich off of their kid's nightmare? It's a different type of child abuse. Can you see them in a network studio office: "We think the country should know all the terrible things that happened to our daughter. America has a right to know the truth." "Okay, just sign right here. Here's your check." We tell our kids, if something happens to you that doesn't feel right, go tell an adult that you trust. I bet her brother and sister are like, "Shit, if something happens to me, I'm gonna keep this terrible-ass secret to myself."

What happened to exploiting our kids through pageants? I'd rather you paint my face and curl my hair than give the world a detailed description of my rape.

Presidential Bushes

The Bush twins caught hell when their dad became president. America thought they had some wild girls in the White House. Jenna and Barbara. They got caught drinking underage, so what? That must suck being the president's kid.

You've got Secret Service following you around, people don't like you because they are pissed at your father's policies, and you've got the Secret Service up your ass. If you're a teenager, the last thing you want is old, stiff men in dark suits following you around. That's how the Bush girl kept getting busted. She would go out to the bar and try to buy alcohol with a fake ID. Now teenagers try to get served all the time; this is not outrageous behavior for a nineteen-year-old. However, it's pretty difficult to pull it off when you have old, stiff men in dark suits with earpieces standing behind you while you're talking to the bartender. What did she say?

Daughter: Can I get a fuzzy navel?

Bartender: Aren't you the president's daughter?

Daughter: No, I'm Lil' Kim. These guys are my body-guards.

That's not too bright. She must take after her daddy.

It must really suck. Your life gets screwed up because your dad wants to be president so he can screw everybody else's life up. It's like being a rock star but not being able to do any of the fun, crazy rock star shit. I bet the Olsen twins have more fun than the Bush twins.

They are in college, so you know all of the college guys are trying to get with them. Come on, that's a prize. Bagging one of the twins will get you in the fraternity. Then again, the way their daddy went after Saddam, it could get your campus bombed, too. No worries, he'll send Haliburton in to rebuild. You know those college guys would love to run back to the dorm: "Hey, man, guess who just blew me? The president's daughter. My dick is presidential. You should salute my dick." Now we know this scenario won't happen, because I'm sure it's hard to keep an erection when you have old, stiff guys in dark suits wearing earpieces and packing guns standing behind the girl who's blowing you.

America didn't have to worry about these types of shenanigans when Chelsea was the first daughter. All that mess she went through, I'm sure sex was not on her agenda. Besides, Chelsea probably got sick and tired of her girlfriends running up to her: "Girl, guess who I just blew? Your daddy. Your daddy's crazy."

Chelsea had it rough. She would probably call up her little friends: "Debbie, would you like to come over for a slumber party?"

"Is your daddy gonna be home? Your daddy is fun. I always have a good time when your daddy is around."

Chelsea is one strong young lady. I have much respect for her. No child at any age wants to even think about her parents having sex. That's one of the big fears, to walk in on your parents doing it doggy style. AHHHH!!! That will scar you for life. I would try to find some new eyes.

Chelsea had to deal with the entire world knowing that her father had his dick in some strange girl's mouth. That's fucked-up. You know she was angry with Bill. She probably still is; I would be. And you know any guy she is with can forget about getting a blow job. That's not going to happen, chief. I would have a tattoo right below my belly button that said NO DICKS ALLOWED ABOVE THIS LINE! I would have a sign right over my headboard that said IF YOU CAN READ THIS SIGN, THEN YOUR PENIS IS TOO CLOSE TO MY MOUTH. I bet if a guy tried to put his penis anywhere near her mouth she'd grab it and twist it up like a balloon animal. It's a penis, now it's an elephant.

Part Nine

Women

Women are so analytical. All we do is think. Think, think, think. Think all the time. Right? Can't stop thinking. Ladies, have you ever remembered a time when you had a moment of silence in your head? No. Of course you don't, and if you did, you're dead. It doesn't happen, does it? No. Always thinking. Sometimes you can't even sleep, because you won't shut the hell up.

You're in the bed, and your mind is just racing about nothing. Just thinking, Mmmm, I need to talk to her tomorrow, because I didn't like the way she spoke to me today. And I'm not gonna have this uncomfortable thing going on between us. Did I lock the door? I should have bought those shoes. Where's my high school yearbook? Oooh, what am I gonna have for lunch tomorrow? Mmm, I don't know. Why am I thinking about lunch? I need to have a good breakfast. That's what I'm gonna do. I'm gonna start every morning with a good breakfast. Maybe I'll start that low-carb diet. That seems to be working for a lot of people. What was my third-grade English teacher's name? What was her name?

Miss Jones? Miss Jenkins? I should get Tivo. I could tape *Oprah* every day. I should get a tattoo. I wonder how many frequent flyer miles I have. I haven't had a tuna fish sandwich in years. I should paint the bathroom. When is Anita Baker gonna put out a new record? Wooo, it's late! I need to be asleep. What the hell am I doin' up? I don't know. Let me think about it.

That's why I envy men. Man, I wish I could think like a guy. Because guys, they don't spend all that time thinking. Men, their process is so different. They think about it, thought about it, moving on. That's it. That's why they enjoy sports. Because you ain't gotta think about it. It's cut and dry. You know, either you got the basket or you didn't. Either you made the touchdown or you didn't.

If there's any question about it, there's a referee right there to sort it all out for them.

Ref: After further review, play stands as called, touchdown. Stop thinking.

Man: Okay, thanks, man. Thank you. Woo. I ain't gotta do all of that thinking.

But women, we think all the time. Sometimes we forget and think that men think as much as we do. Guys, have you ever been quiet for a minute around your girl? What's the first thing we ask? "What are you thinking?" And guys always reply with the same thing, "Nothing." Ladies, *believe* them!

They can actually do that. Leave the man alone. If you keep bugging him, he's gonna be thinking, Will you shut the fuck up? *That's* what I was thinking.

That's a Dumb Idea . . . Period!

I don't do period jokes, but my friend Alyson brought something to my attention that just put me over the edge. Also I need to turn in seventy thousand words for this book. Like I said, I don't do period jokes, but something needs to be said about how these companies treat women like we're mindless.

I told my good friend Alyson, a talented writer, that she could use this space in my book to get the following off of her chest, as long as she could do it in a thousand words. *Ladies and Gentlemen: Please welcome to my book, the very funny and talented, Alyson Fouse.*

Thanks, Wanda. Last month when I was having a bad three to five days, I noticed that Kotex was printing little helpful tips on the back of their maxipads. "Tips for Life" is what they call them. I call them a dumb idea. It's a sanitary napkin, not a fortune cookie. Besides, the time you're most likely to see these "tips" is not really when you're open for suggestions.

Excuse me, Alyson, for interrupting, but you know how I loathe period-related material, so could you not say "sanitary napkin"? Yuck.

Well, Wanda, what the fuck else would you like for me to call it, a bloody wad of cotton?

Never mind.

Let me set up the scenario. Ladies, say you're stuck in a long and tedious staff meeting where no one listens to your ideas because you're a woman, and the only doughnut left is that ashy chocolate cake one with the dried-up coconut sprinkles. Who are we fooling? You know you're going to eat it anyway, because you were running late for work on account of the Motrin you took the night before for your cramps knocked you out like you were Mike Tyson's sparring partner, or ex-wife. It's possible the label on the bottle was right, you shouldn't have taken two pills with alcohol, but is wine really considered alcohol?

Not in my book.

Wanda . . .

I'm sorry, continue.

And since you already had a couple of glasses, you might as well finish off the whole bottle. Right? Or is that just me? Anyway, your long-winded, balding boss with more hair coming out of his nose than the top of his head is finally wrapping up his report and everybody gets up to leave.

Everybody but you, that is, because you have to be the last one out of your chair just in case you left enough DNA on it for somebody to mistake it for a crime scene.

So you smile politely, and shuffle your papers. Then tell that girlfriend who takes every break, lunch, and walk out to the parking lot after work to talk about other coworkers and their kids, that you'll catch up, and she doesn't get it. But other people (mostly men) are still in the room so you can't tell her that you might be sitting on possible evidence that will confirm their suspicions that you really are a woman. Instead you try to give her the eye and maybe she'll receive the message telepathically. But she's not Jean Grey from the X-Men. She can't read your fucking mind. She just thinks you have an attitude and leaves. Now you've got to buy her lunch and explain over fajitas that you weren't mad at her, but you were mad at your life-giving womb that you wish would just fall out already.

Uh, Alyson—

Wanda, would you shut the fuck up?

Jeez . . . okay . . . somebody's on the rag.

Nevertheless, you're finally alone and the only thing left in your seat are crumbs from the doughnut that you swear you'll spend a full forty-five minutes on the treadmill for, but know damn well you won't. Is it really a lie if you only tell it to yourself? Only if God hears you. And He's not listening anyway, because you cursed Him out last night for those cramps. Which are starting to kick back in to remind you that this shit was aptly coined when they referred to it as a fucking curse. Which is what you do all the way to the ladies' room, because for some reason everybody is in your gotdamn way. Don't these people have shit to do? Luckily, you finally make it and get everything situated. I won't go into details about what goes where, but ladies, after the morning you've been through, the last thing you want to do is read the back of your pad. Especially when it's something dumb, like, "Drinking eight glasses of water a day will help you to feel fresh." Or "Avoiding caffeine may help reduce cramps and headaches." Even better, "Staying active during your period can help relieve cramps." Fuck you, Kotex. Why don't you give us some "tips" we can really use, like, "How to dispose of your husband's body." Or "What to put in your kids' cereal to make them take a seventy-two-hour nap." And what we all want to know is, "Why didn't they mention any of this shit in *Are You There, God? It's Me, Margaret?*" Better yet, "Will there be a menopause edition entitled *Lord, Jesus! Put Down the Gun, Maggie?*" There'd better be. Otherwise, if I ever meet Judy Blume I'ma punch her right in the face. That bitch fooled us all. She's one of the reasons there's too much misleading information out there. That's why I'm going to give you some *real* tips for life:

1. When you're feeling crabby, spread it around. You'll feel better when you fuck up everybody else's day.

2. When you can't stand the sight of your husband, leave him.

3. Smoking a joint helps to relieve the pain of everything.

4. If monthly cramps are a bother, have a hysterectomy.

5. Fighting fatigue with crack usually helps you get through the day.

6. Eating five helpings of fruits and vegetables will give you so much gas, you'll forget all about your period.

7. Water only curbs your cravings for more water. Have the damn chocolate.

8. When your body temperature rises, strip down to your granny panties and tell the world to kiss your fat ass.

9. Mood swings will often pass with a good cry and a bottle of tequila.

10. Don't let bloating keep you from wearing your favorite jeans. Loop a rubber band over the button and through the hole, then tell everyone it's in style.

See, now those are some tips you can use, and we need not ever talk about our periods again. Thank you.

Alyson Fouse, everybody! Let her hear it. Thanks, Alyson. One thousand, one hundred and fourteen words, good job!

The Article

My publicist called to tell me that *Esquire* magazine wanted me to do an article entitled "Ten Things You Didn't Know About Women." I thought it would be fun, so I accepted. Of course, being the procrastinator that I am, I was sweating, trying to beat the end-of-the-day deadline during lunch with Sue and Alyson, who you just met, a couple of my girlfriends who are also writers. I jokingly said something like, "The way to a woman's heart is through her clit." My friends fell out laughing and quickly jumped on the clit bandwagon. They talked me into doing this list. I actually submitted this to *Esquire*.

1. The quickest way to a woman's heart is through her clit.
2. When we say we want you to get in touch with your feminine side, we really mean you need to touch our clits.
3. When we ask you if we look fat, it really means, "Can you see my clit?"
4. We'd love to meet your mom. Right after we introduce you to our clits.
5. Diamonds are forever, but touching our clits can buy ya two or three years.

6. When we tell you, "We're not communicating," it really means you're not touching our clits.

7. We'd be happy to buy our own damn drinks, if you touch our clits.

8. When we say, "Harder! Harder!" that means, "Take it out and touch my clit."

9. The fact that women make seventy-five cents to every man's dollar won't bother us . . . as long as you touch our clits.

10. "Go have a boys' night out" really means, "I'll stay home and touch my clit."

I know, very funny. The person at *Esquire* didn't think so. I got another call from my publicist.

Publicist: Wanda, about that article, I really wished that you had sent it to me before sending it right in to *Esquire.*

Me: (through a laugh) What's the problem?

Publicist: Esquire feels that it's a little too uh . . . racy . . . uh, edgy for them to publish.

Me: What do you mean?

Publicist: Okay, to be honest, it's just too much clit. I mean, like every joke is clit.

Me: What's wrong with clit? I think this article could be very helpful to some guys.

Publicist: Uh, yeah, but it's just too much clit. You need to do another pass at this. One, maybe two clit jokes are fine, but the entire list of clit lines is just overkill.

Me: Oh, I think one or two clit lines would just come across as tacky and vulgar.

Publicist: Okay, well, do another list without any clit at all.

After being lectured about the clit article by my publicist, I came up with a watered-down version. My publicist was delighted.

1. Writing poetry makes us look for your other homosexual tendencies.

    You write us a beautiful poem. We think this is pretty and sensitive. Wait, this is pretty. What the fuck? What else is pretty about this man? If a man's gonna express his feelings, he should write dirty poetry. Why sugarcoat it with all that mushy stuff?

2. If women were physically stronger than men, we'd kick your ass every day.

3. You've never talked your way into our pants. We made that decision when we met you. However, if we're wearing shabby underwear, we hadn't planned on sleeping with you that day.

4. Why do we fake orgasms? It's called time management.

5. After sex, you can gauge your performance by the

temperature of the washcloth we bring you. If it's warm, you were great. If it's cold, we've had better. If you have to get it yourself, don't bother coming back to bed.

6. Being a sports fan is cool, but we think guys who paint their faces are closeted drag queens.

7. We think the Three Stooges are funny, too, just for different reasons.

8. We really aren't bad drivers. We're just trying to ruin your day.

9. It is about money and power. Donald Trump driving a bus, he's ignored. Donald Trump standing in front of his casino, he's a handsome fella.

10. We don't like it when you cry. Be a man, dammit!

Clearly this version didn't hit the sweet spot like the Clit version. And I wasn't the only one who noticed. I received a message from my publicist: "The editor in chief likes the clit version." I said, "Great!! We have something in common." Then the conversation went something like this:

Publicist: I think you should go with the second version. The one without all of the clit.

Me: But it's not as funny. Anybody could have written that boring shit. The clit is me.

Publicist: But you don't want to be known as the "clit

woman." I don't want you on every talk show being asked about your clit.

Me: It's a good icebreaker.

Publicist: It's your call. My advice, don't go with the clit.

Me: I gotta go with my gut and it's feeling clit.

The Orlando Jones Show was the only interview that I did where I was asked about this article.

How to Ruin Porn

I know you guys are going, "Why in the world would you want to do that?" Well, fellas, some of us ladies are not big fans of the porn. It's not that I'm a prude or anything. I'm just more of a film buff. When I watch a "movie," I pay attention to the dialogue, the performance, the direction, the cinematography, wardrobe, I watch it all. I can't watch a movie for the sheer fucking. All of the other things that are lacking get in the way and I just find the whole thing funny. So I laugh. Yes, if you pop a porn in, the only reaction that you are getting out of me is giggles. You might as well turn on Nick at Nite, you'll get the same response, laughs. Ladies, guys hate that. If you want to score points, don't laugh during the porn watching.

However, if you're like me and want to put an end to the porn watching, warm-up part of the sex festivities, laugh. Plus, I don't need it. Hey, I love football, but I really don't need to see the pregame. Guys, to me your porn watching is like our postgame cuddling; you don't need it, nor do you look forward to it.

Last guy I was with, I just got fed up with the porn watching. So instead of laughing, I decided to break him. If you want to ruin porn, ladies, follow the scenario that I played out. The two of you are watching some porn, you are stroking him, then stop and point to the TV screen.

You: Look at that dick! I have never seen a dick that big before in my life. Are they supposed to be that big?

Him: Oh, uh . . . uh . . . don't pay any attention to that. They do that with uh . . . uh . . . that's just lights and shit.

You: Lights? Hmmm . . . we need to get some lights up in here. Floodlights, flashlights, strobe lights, Christmas lights, candlelight, lightning bugs, I don't care; we just need some lights up in this bitch.

This is when he gets pissed.

Him: Well, look at her titties. Man, she has some nice, big ol' titties. That's a lucky man right there.

You: Lucky? Shit, he deserves those titties. Look at that big-ass dick!

After that, the next movie you guys watch together will be *Finding Nemo.* Still give him shit: "Nemo's daddy is sexy."

More Advice . . . for Her

After the "Ten Things You Don't Know About Women" *Esquire* article, Alyson and I were talking about how most of the magazines for women give the worst advice. It's almost as if these writers have never actually met a man. The things they tell women to do are just ridiculous. The only thing I got from these articles is that these people know absolutely nothing about men. Men are not complex at all. Ladies, there's not much to know. My girl Alyson is back to hook y'all up with a very simple way to get you a man. *Take it away, Alyson.*

TEN WAYS TO SEDUCE A MAN
1. Wash your hair with an exotic floral-scented shampoo, then tell him you want to fuck him.
2. In fresh red and pink rose petals, spell out "I want to fuck you."

3. Put on your sexiest dress, then pull it up over your head and tell him you want to fuck him.

4. Spend hours in the kitchen cooking his favorite meal, then tell him you want to fuck him.

5. Cuddle up in front of the television and put in your favorite romantic movie. *Sleepless in Seattle* is always a good choice. Then tell him you want to fuck him.

6. Surprise him during halftime with your own special cheer. It should go something like this: "I want to fuck you."

7. Put the kids to bed early, then tell him you want to fuck him. This is especially seductive if those ain't his kids.

8. Take a stripper class. Then once you bust your ass sliding down that pole, tell him you want to fuck him.

9. Bust all the windows out of his car, then on the side spray-paint, "I want to fuck you."

10. Say hello, then tell him you want to fuck him.

Alyson, I don't know if the girls have caught on yet. Can you help them out? I mean, they've been misled for decades.

Sure.

11. Step on his foot, then tell him you want to fuck him.

12. Find a common interest like . . . you want to fuck him.

13. Spanish is considered to be a very romantic lan-

guage. Learn some Spanish phrases, then tell him, "I want to fuck you, señor."

14. Answer the door wrapped in cellophane, then tell him as soon as you get that shit off your sweaty ass you want to fuck him.

15. Fuck his brother to show just how much you want to fuck him.

16. Take his dick out of your mouth, then tell him you want to fuck him.

17. Accept the speeding ticket, then tell him you want to fuck him.

18. Say you voted for him, then tell him you want to fuck him.

19. Show up at his job wearing nothing but pumps and a trench coat. Then after he's fired, you'll have all day to tell him you want to fuck his unemployed ass.

20. Ask him if he likes pussy. Then depending on his answer, tell him you want to fuck him.

Thanks, Alyson.

Sugar and Spice

Growing up we are all taught that little girls are made up of sugar and spice and everything nice. Guys, I know you want to believe that us girls are sweet and sensitive, but you know we're evil, right? Hey, cayenne pepper is also a spice. It will burn you up inside. Most of us try to put up that front of being ladylike and all soft, but deep down we are some dark creatures. Guys, I'm going to give you a little peek into our minds, give you just a glimpse of how we see shit.

Do you know that if we were physically stronger than you, we'd kick your ass every day? Yes, every single day you'd get an ass-whupping. That's why God gave y'all the muscles. He knew we'd go crazy with them. We'd whup your ass. I don't know how many times a day, but all women have at least one experience where a man does or says something stupid or condescending and all we think is, Man, I wish I could beat his punk ass right now. If I had the strength to beat him within a breath of his life, Lord knows I would do it. We would lose our minds. We would just fight guys for no reason. "Look at his stupid ass; I'm gonna go break his legs."

If things were the other way around and women were in control, guys, you still wouldn't be able to vote. "Who gives a fuck about how you feel on the issues? Shut up before I bust your lip."

Well, guys, there's just a little peek. I can't tell you more because it might mess up the revolution. Oops, I said too much.

Workplace

I don't know if there's something about the tone of our voices or what, but sometimes the few female writers on staff will pitch something and I'll hear it, but the men will keep talking. And one of them will pitch what she already pitched. Then they'll all say, "Yeah, that's a good idea." This would drive them nuts.

I thought it was kinda funny listening to them bitch. "Did you see what just happened in there? I'm so excited that he was able to recite my idea word for word. I should take him everywhere I go. I bet I'd get what I wanted more often with him around. That asshole in front of me at the game would finally move, my friends would go see the movie of *my* choice for a change, and I could visit a celebrity's hotel room after one in the morning. I could just have him yell, 'Don't rape me!!'"

I don't know if it's a woman's tone of voice or that men are just trained to tune us out. Maybe guys are like, "When I go home, I have to hear it. I don't want to hear that shit at work, too." When they get home, they have to listen to their wives because that's who they fuck. They don't listen to us at work because deep down they feel that we don't belong there. I think this goes on in male-dominated fields, like a writers' room. Men don't expect to hear a female voice in the room so they ignore it. They just don't hear us. However, there were some benefits, too; the female writers could fart in the room and none of the guys would hear it.

My Right

I believe in a woman's right to choose. First of all, I don't think it's any of my business to tell another woman what to do with her body. I'll leave that up to Joan and Melissa Rivers. You can't make somebody be a mother if they don't want to be a mother. The same way you can't make a man be a father if he doesn't want to be a father. Yeah, if you're lucky you can get a monthly support check from him, but that's about it. He doesn't even have to see the lil' bastard if he chooses not to be involved. It all falls on the woman. That's why when you see news reports about the police finding a four-year-old child left alone in an apartment for a week, it's always the mother who went to Vegas with her new boyfriend. Mommy was feeling lucky and they don't allow kids on the casino floor.

I know the opponents of the right to choose feel that abortions are morally wrong. They feel that abortions are murder of the unborn and go against their Christian beliefs, blah, blah, blah. I can understand that, but I believe the real drive is that they want to have control, especially men. It drives men nuts that they don't even have a say in something so monumental as giving birth. Remember, there was a time not too long ago when women couldn't even vote.

What gets me going is the Right to Lifers act like the pro-choice people are really pro-abortionist. There isn't a woman out there who is proud to have an abortion. Like we're out having abortion parties. "Hey, bartender, my girl Jenny had an abortion today. Body shots!" It's ridiculous. Hallmark doesn't make greeting cards, "Congrats on Your Abortion," or "Heard It Was a Boy."

An abortion is a personal and private, unfortunate situation that should be between a woman, her doctor, and her God. That's why all women lie about them. It's none of your business. A woman will lie to you about an abortion in a minute. Anytime a woman has to fill out a medical history form, I guarantee you that the abortion is not getting checked. "Shit, what does that abortion I had two years ago have to do with a teeth cleaning? No." It's none of your business. We will lie like we're at a congressional hearing. Sometimes we lie so much that it is forgotten. We block it out of our memory. We could be on the table about to have an abortion . . .

> *Doctor:* You checked here that you've never had an abortion.
>
> *Woman:* Right.
>
> *Doctor:* I performed an abortion on you last December.
>
> *Woman:* Naw, wasn't me.

When it comes to an abortion, women are like Nazis when it comes to the Holocaust: It never happened.

If Roe v. Wade was overturned, I know one person who would be dancing in the streets, Maury Povich. Yep, *The Maury Povich Show* has turned into the *Who's Your Baby's Daddy Show*. If you don't know your baby's father, go visit Maury. He'll give everybody a DNA test to find that man. This one pitiful woman was making her fifth appearance on the show looking for her baby's daddy. Maury had tested fourteen men and none of them were the father. I think it's so irresponsible to not be able to pinpoint who fathered your child. I mean, it should be simple. "Let's see, who did I fuck in May?" Fourteen dudes, fourteen possibles. What was she doing, fucking in her sleep? "Maury, I'm a sleep fucker. I can't count the number of mornings I woke up with my panties off and my legs over my head." That's just nasty.

Baby Love

My ex-husband was quite a few years younger than me. I figured if you can't find a good man, raise one. Although I believed the age discrepancy wasn't that big of a deal, we were at totally different stages in our lives. He would come home with good news like, so-and-so got married or so-and-so just had their first baby. I would come home with news like, so-and-so has cancer or so-and-so just passed away from a heart attack. After a few years in the relationship, he admitted that there were times when he woke up next to me thinking I was dead.

One time, I woke up to him giving me CPR.

> *Him:* One and two and three and four and . . .
>
> *Me:* I'm not dead, dummy!
>
> *Him:* My bad, baby, you just had one of those faraway looks on your face. And you looked so peaceful.

One time I came home drunk, slurring my speech, making no sense, and bumping into things as most drunks do. I heard him tell his friends he thought I was showing early stages of Alzheimer's disease.

When we'd go on vacation, he'd want to ride jet skis; I'd want to get a nap by the pool. I guess when you reach a certain age you don't even entertain the idea of doing something that if it goes wrong it could be life threatening. You figure if you've made it this far, you gotta save what life you got left.

Strip Classes

All these women are taking stripper classes in hopes their men will stop going to strip clubs. First of all, you can't compete with those strippers. Stripping is a lifestyle. You gotta have the stripper clothes, the stripper perfume, the stripper language, and most of all, the stripper mentality. In other words, the ability to lie like a dog for a measly buck. A stripper will tell your man anything for a dollar. "Oow, I thought you were Brad Pitt."

These stripper classes are very popular. Women are getting poles installed in their bedrooms or basements. Your man will play along and I'm sure he appreciates your efforts. Hell, he might even put a dollar bill in the crack of your ass, but that's not keeping him out of the clubs. It's not the same thing. Hey, I'll go to my nephew's Little League game, cheer him on, buy him a Happy Meal after the game. But I'm still going to watch the Yankees. You can't beat the pros. The main thing that women don't get, men like going to strip clubs because you're not there!

I guess what really annoys me about these classes is that it seems so needy. You're literally bending over backward for his ass. He ain't thinking about what he could do to please you or how to make himself more attractive for you. I was at a party and this woman started handing out her "I teach strip classes" card. She gave me one. I ripped that shit up before she could get it out of her hand good. Women do some silly-ass, demeaning shit. I was laughing at all of them, and I guess that vodka I was drinking saw the humor, too. I was like, "What is wrong with y'all? Fuck him. Do you think your man is out at some club or at the gym and another dude comes in handing out his card? 'Hey, man, come to my pussy-lickin' class. Your lady will thank you.' 'Hey, come to my ball-washing seminar; the ladies will appreciate it.'" No! He ain't thinking about your pole-swirling ass. Women do some stupid shit.

Part Ten

"Ruff, Ruff"

You ever notice that whenever you get at least two women together, during the conversation one of them is going to say, "Men are dogs"? You hear it all the time, talk shows, dating shows, courtrooms, church, and usually right before, "Please, baby, don't shoot!" I think calling men "dogs" is unfair. They aren't dogs. I think they are just men. They can't help it.

Men are not dogs. Why? Because I trust my dog. Come on, guys, I never found any strange panties in my dog's car. My dog has never run up my phone bill calling some nine hundred number to talk dirty to some nasty ho. My dog has never had another master and family across town that he was hiding. No. Men are not dogs. Dogs are loyal, they protect you, and they can lick their own balls.

Guy Tip One

Here's a tip for you guys. When a woman asks you to do something and prefaces it with "when you get a chance," or "when you get around to it," just stop what you're doing and do the shit right then and there. When we ask, we really don't mean when you get a chance, when you feel like it, or when you get around to it. No, we mean right now. If you do it, you'll save yourself a lot of time and grief and a lot of arguments.

We say "when you get a chance," because we don't want to sound like we're nagging you, so we make you think that you have an option to do whatever it is at your convenience. You really don't.

Guys, I know you've been there. You're watching the game. She comes in . . .

Wife: Baby, I was out gardening and noticed that the gutters are a little clogged up, so when you get a chance could you clean the gutters out? You know, when you feel like it.

Husband: Yeah, sure, no problem.

So you continue to watch the game because, fellas, you'll clean the gutters when you get a chance. Twenty minutes later you hear footsteps, or more like somebody stomping on the roof. You go outside and her crazy ass is on top of the roof pulling crap out of the gutters that she asked you to clean when you got a chance.

Wife: I asked you to do just one thing, one thing and you don't do it. You don't do shit in the house. You don't do shit outside the house. All you wanna do is sit on your lazy, good-for-nothing ass and watch that damn TV. I hate you. You sorry bastard.

Guys, don't try to stop her; it's too late. Just hang your head like the lazy bastard you've been called, turn around and go back into the house, get your car keys, and get the hell out of there.

This is how women operate. It's passed down from generation to generation. I learned it at a very early age. I remember on Saturday mornings when my brother and I would be watching cartoons, my mother would ask us to do chores around the house.

Mom: Hey, when you get a chance, could you kids vacuum the living room? We're having company over later.
Us: Sure, Mom.

Which really meant, "Get out of the way and get your face out of Pufnstuf's ass." We'd just stare at the TV and think,

She said when we get a chance. Ten minutes later, Mom would come in, vacuum cleaner blazin'. She'd vacuum everything, just fuckin' up the TV reception. We couldn't see shit! She would be fussin' and cussin', but we couldn't really hear what she was saying over the noise from the vacuum. I still jump whenever I hear a vacuum cleaner.

Guy Tip Two

We talk all the time. But it's so hard for us to articulate exactly what we want, what we need, what we feel. Do you know how hard it is for us to be direct? It's taught to us, because if we are direct we run the risk of being called a bitch. Right? So we gotta be a little tricky. Gotta be a little slick. Right? Instead of coming out and just telling you something or asking you something, we'd rather give you a test. Oh, we are some testing people, aren't we? Boy, SATs ain't got nothing on us. Women will give you a test.

Fellas, do you know that we fail you at tests that you don't even know you're taking? Failing miserably. You're getting a big F, and don't even know the test is in progress.

How unfair is that? We test on everything, simple stuff, too. Okay, here's the situation.

A guy gets home first and there are a few dishes in the sink. He doesn't even bother washing the dishes. He chills reading the paper or maybe sneaks some porn time in or whatever. His girl comes home, sees the dishes, and sees him chilling. She ain't gonna say anything, but it gets downloaded. She's gonna create a little folder. Gonna be a little icon with his face on it. And it's gonna say, "Dishes." And she puts it right up there on the desktop of her mental computer screen.

Three more days and that same mess goes on. She comes home, sees him chilling, dishes in the sink. She just opens the file to store more info about his sorry ass. However, that fourth day, she comes home, sees him chilling. She's gonna double-click right on his face. *Click-click.* Open up the folder. "Let me think about what this man is trying to tell me. What is he saying? Is he trying to tell me that I'm the little dish-washer around here? Huh? Is he telling me that washing dishes, that's beneath him? Because you know what? I work every day, too. Maybe I'd like to come home to a clean sink, and go start my evening—you know what? I was not put on this earth to wash his dirty dishes. I tell you what. I'm not gonna wash another damn dish. And I'm gonna see how long he's gonna let these dishes pile up before he'll wash them."

He doesn't even know the test is going on. Three weeks go by. Now she's so pissed she can't even see straight because they're walking around the house eating off of napkins with toothpicks. Ain't a damn thing clean in the house. And he don't care, because he's like, "Shit, this is how I lived before I met your ass. Welcome to my world." Oh, but it doesn't end there, does it? Oh, no. Uh-uh. He's just at the gates of hell right now. He ain't in the fire yet. No.

Because with women, something that we're pissed about in the kitchen is gonna walk its way right down the hallway into the bedroom. And guys don't know. They have no idea. So he gets in the bed, trying to be all intimate, trying to get a little something going on. He's doing his little poking thing. He's in there behaving like an A student, not knowing he got a big-ass F. He's in there poking and she just snaps on his ass. And now, he's in the bed with cracked ribs. And he's like, "What the hell is your problem? What's wrong with you?" And she looks at him like he's a stranger. "What, what, what, what is my problem? *What's my problem?* You're just all energy tonight, huh? Oh, you're just bubbling with energy. You're in here rubbing on me and touching my ass. But you can't wash a muthafuckin' glass? Why don't I go sit in the dish rack, see if you notice me then, huh? Get off me."

Door Number Two

I've dated all types. I must say, a cheap date can be good for a few laughs, that is, if you can afford them. The cheap dates always cloak themselves as romantics. They like doing things like going on long walks, visiting a museum, reading you poetry, bike riding, you know? Free shit. They love taking you on dates that don't cost a thing. I remember this one dude used to give me one rose, and he had a corny line to go along with it, "I give you one rose because you are one special lady." After a couple of dates I was like, "No, you give me one rose because you are one cheap bastard." My all-time favorite cheap date happened during the time I lived in New Jersey. He used to back up to the toll so that the booth would be on my side.

The Drive

Studies show that men think about sex all the time. Did they really need to do a study to figure that shit out? Pornography is a billion-dollar industry. I don't think men are supporting it for fashion suggestions. I think it's a waste of time for women to keep complaining about how men "just want sex." "They think with their dicks."

That crazy sex drive, it's something in men. It's part of their makeup. It's innate. I believe it is part of the plan. It had to be that way. That's why we still have people walking around on this earth. Men are baby makers, so they are always in that mode, "We gotta make more people. We gotta make more people."

Women have the people, so we're like, "Wait, who's gonna take care of all these people? Get off me."

Number One Fantasy

The number one fantasy for most guys is a threesome. They want to have two women at the same time. I think that's a bit lofty. If you can't satisfy that one woman, why do you want to piss off another one? Why have two angry women in the bedroom with you at the same time?

And guys, think about it—you know how much you hate to talk after sex. Imagine having two women just nagging you to death. "So what are you thinking? Come on, let's talk." The other one says, "Hold me. We never cuddle."

Men can watch two women together and that's a turn-on. It doesn't work the same way for us ladies. You ask any woman her sexual fantasy and I bet you a million dollars it won't be to go home and see your man bent over with some big, burly guy standing behind him smacking his ass, yelling, "Oh yeah. Say my name. Who's your daddy?" Oh, that will ruin your day.

Feeling Twenty-six

I still feel and think the same way I did when I was twenty-six. I feel twenty-six. Especially after I have a few drinks. Oh, boy. Then it really kicks in. Right, ladies? You feel sexy when you drink. I'm thinking, I knew I was twenty-six. I don't know what that lying-ass calendar was talking about. I'm twenty-six.

You're at the bar, talking trash. Then you go to the ladies' room, and you check yourself out in the mirror. You're like, "You're a sexy bitch. You little sexy— I'd fuck you."

I went down to South Beach with four girlfriends.

Hanging out in Miami on South Beach, drinking with our little thong bikinis on, letting it all hang out, feeling sexy, feeling twenty-six, until some real twenty-six-year-olds walk by. I had to put my drink down. "Pass me my sarong. It got windy out here, didn't it?" Yeah, a little twenty-six-year-old wind just whipped through and blew my ass back to the real world.

I Feel Sexy

See, women love feeling sexy. Men like having sex. There's a big difference. See, men don't understand the difference between feeling sexy and not having sex. That doesn't make any sense to them. They're like, "Okay, wait a minute, okay, you feel sexy but you don't want to have sex? Oh, that's just impossible. I don't understand that; that makes absolutely no sense." Guys believe that you can't feel any sexier than when you're having sex. That's the epitome of feeling sexy to guys. Guys are like, "Baby, you just don't know how sexy you look in that doggy position. I'm telling you. So sexy! I've never seen you so sexy. And the way the light from the TV hits the side of your face. Oh, baby."

100 Percent Pure Sex

I don't blame guys for being horny all the time, because when you just look at the act of sex, guys got it made. They really do. Every time a man has sex he's going to complete the act. For guys, sex is like going to a restaurant. No matter what you order off the menu, you walk out of there going, "Damn, that was good. Woooo! She put something special on that." As he rubs his stomach, he says, "Ah, good, my compliments to the chef. Good Lord, that was tasty. Man, I want to hit this three, four times a day. I love this."

Women, it doesn't work like that for us. We go to the restaurant and order something. Sometimes it's good. Sometimes you gotta send it back. Sometimes you might get food poisoning. You keep having those hits and misses. You're gonna want to skip a few meals, right? "Oh no, I'm not hungry today. I was thinking about starting my fast. I think now is a good time." Or you may go, "Ya know, I think I may cook for myself today. It's just something about the way I cook. I mean, it's always filling. I mean, my cooking sticks to your ribs! I just love the way I cook, and ya know what? I'm a fast cook, I tell ya. I can whip 'em up. By the time it takes you to do one meal, I can make three!"

But guys get satisfaction every time. That must be wonderful going into it, knowing that you're about to have a pleasurable sexual experience. That is amazing, because women have to get in the middle of it before we actually figure out if the train's going to pull into the station or not. You're there holding your bags, looking up the tracks, praying to see the light from the train; shit, you'll be happy just to hear the engine or a whistle blow.

And then guys wonder why we fake it. It's called time management. Ain't no need to be up all night working on something when I know there's been a derailment up ahead. I don't need to be up all night working on something I know ain't gonna happen. You're just cutting into my sleep time now. Shoot, I tried to do us both a favor. Guys, don't get your feelings hurt, just roll over and go to sleep.

Every woman has been in that situation. He's working hard trying to make it happen when you already know it ain't gonna happen. You glance over at the clock and you're like, "Shoot, it's one thirty in the morning! And I gotta get up at six. One thirty, two thirty, three thirty, four thirty, five thirty six thirty, oh, to hell with this. Ohhhh, yes, woooow, ohhhh, yes, baby, wooow, ooooh, Yes! Hercules, Hercules, Hercules, Hercules, Hercules, Hercules!"

Captain of the Vessel

I don't need much in the bedroom. I appreciate the basics. Touch that, lick this, put that there . . . I'm cool. As a matter of fact, I hate those artistic fucks. You know, the ones where you feel like it's been choreographed. Where you expect to see Debbie Allen standing in the corner, "And, one, two, three, legs up!" That shit gets on my nerves. I'm not gonna burn all of that energy until you prove to me that you know how to please me. If I burn two hours in the bed with you and at the end of the session I haven't had a single, solitary orgasm, I'm ready to fight. You can get the hell out. Shit, I would have been better off spending that time at the gym. At least I would have lost a few pounds and maybe been able to attract somebody who knows how to fuck.

I enjoy sex, but to me there is a goal involved that we both should be striving for. Now if I know and you know how to reach that goal, why tinker with perfection? I don't think I'm boring in bed. I like to consider myself efficient. If you're doing something that I know isn't working for me, I'll let you stray for a few minutes, but then I'm going to get us back on course. I'm the captain of this vessel. You know if the ship is on course, the captain is usually below in his cabin chilling. The crew is taking care of business. Like the captain, I only pop up on deck when there's a problem. "Hey, we're sinking. This ain't the *Titanic*, muthafucka. Bail! Bail!"

I don't like food mixed in with my sex, either. I'm not putting whipped cream on nothing. If you don't like it plain, then kiss my ass and get out. Plus, everything doesn't agree with my stomach. A banana split sitting in my gut is seriously going to affect my performance. What's wrong with good, old-fashioned sex? Edible panties, that's some bullshit. This country is fat enough already, now we got to have a snack during sex, too?

As you can see, I'm an impatient mu'fucka. So I let you know up front, if you know how to please me, just stick with that. Don't get fancy on me; stay the course that gets me there. Don't try some new route that you don't know shit about, because now you're just going to get all lost, fumbling around. And just like a man, you're not going to stop and ask for directions. No, you're just going to keep going until you run out of gas. Leaving me stranded in the middle of the ocean, not even a breeze blowing for the sails. Now I gotta row just to get myself there.

Part Eleven

Moving to the Left

The most difficult adjustment moving to Los Angeles is dealing with all this damn driving. To get anywhere in L.A., you gotta drive. You have to drive somewhere if you want to go for a walk. I hate all that damn driving because it interferes with my drinking. See, this is why I love me some New York. You have the ability to drink to your fullest potential in New York because of all the public transportation and those beautiful cabs. In L.A. I've seen bus stops and people at them waiting, but I haven't seen a bus yet. I don't think they exist.

But in New York, I just love the fact that all you need is five dollars in your pocket and your address pinned to your collar and you get home. All you have to do to get that cab is stand at the curb and raise one arm . . . and make sure your black male friend is out of sight. When I'm in New York, I'm at the bar drinking, the bartender comes over, "Uh—can I get you another one?" If I can still raise my arm: "Oh, yeah. I could have about two more." Because in New York—that's all you have to be able to do. Just wander your ass to that curb, and raise your arm.

When you're out drinking and you know you gotta drive, you try to be responsible, right? You do. You have good intentions. You tell yourself, you say, Okay, I'm driving tonight. I'm gonna have two drinks. That's it. That's what you say. But when you get with your friends, that type of reasoning goes right out the window. Because your friends, they want you to act an ass, too. Everybody has to be drunk; those are the rules. You don't want somebody sober, recalling the events the next day. You don't want to hear, "Girl, you peed on yourself." "What? I did not. You make me sick. I hate hanging out with your sober ass."

You want everybody drunk. That's why no matter what you do—if you go, "No, no. Two drinks, man. I'm—I'm done," you always get the one friend that'll go, "No, no, no. Come on, man. Have another drink. You'll be all right. I'll follow you home." And we all fall for that for some reason, right? I never understood the logic behind that, exactly. It's like, okay, I'm gonna get my drunk ass in my car. And you're gonna get your drunk ass in your car. And we're gonna have this drunk caravan just flying down the highway.

How does having a drunk behind you improve your driving? But we all do it. The only thing that's good for is when you crash. Your drunk friend will be there to tell the cops what happened.

Drunk: Ooh, Officer, I saw the whole thing. It was tragic. Okay, this is what happened, right? Can you get that light out of my eye, Officer? Oh, no you can't? Well, okay. This is what happened. Now you see how the road goes this way? Well, she went that way. I was following her until she hit that tree. And then, I said, "Well, maybe she lives in the woods. Maybe she got a tree house. Maybe she bakes chocolate chip cookies with those little elves." Hey, easy with the cuffs.

They Take Your Car

Several states have strict laws to crack down on drunk drivers. In New York, if the cops pull you over and they think that you've been drinking, they can take your car. They don't even have to test you. If they think you've been drinking, you're walking home. I live in New York. I sold my car, to hell with that bullshit. I had a nice car, too. I sold my car and bought ten shitty cars. Hey, they weren't going to catch me out there. And with me, the cops wouldn't even have to think about if I had been drinking. I probably would've had a glass on the dashboard.

So now it's like, "Okay, you got me. No, no, no, Officer. It's fine. Take my car. I have nine more. That's right. I have a fleet of shitty cars. I'm proud of them, too. I have personalized tags that say SHITTY 1, SHITTY 2, 2SHITTY4U, SHTFLW-BYU, IBSHITTY. I have a bumper sticker that says, *My other car is just as shitty.*

Free Drinks

When I was married, I didn't go out with my single friends because I never had a good time. We'd go to a club and a guy would come over to me, "Hey, can I buy you a drink?" They're like, "Oh, no. She's married." I was like, "Yeah, I'm married, but I'm thirsty. Why don't you shut the hell up? Let me have a free drink." Women love free drinks. We do. They taste better when you don't pay for them. But I noticed something; guys don't buy drinks like they used to. This feminist shit is starting to backfire. Remember the good old days when the bartender would come over and say, "Excuse me, the gentlemen over there in the corner would like to buy you a drink." "Okay, beautiful." You would get your drink and the kind gentleman would do the greatest thing of all. He would keep his ass way over there in the corner and leave you the hell alone. He would let you enjoy your vodka tonic in private. All you had to do was shake your drink at him and mouth, "Thank you." Then smiling through clenched teeth, you'd say, "Stay over there. Don't bring your ass over here." Guys don't do that now. A guy buys you a drink and it gives him the right to stalk you for the rest of the night. He's in your face before the drink gets there. You know that guy.

Guy: How you doin', girl?

Me: Fine. Thanks for the drink.

Guy: Yeah, you can call me Drink Man. What's your name?

Me: Wanda.

Guy: Wanda. Wanda, Wanda. I'm *wanda*-ring how you gonna pay me back for that drink later on.

You go to the ladies' room and he's there leaning against the sink, like he's the bathroom attendant.

Jerk: Well, well, well, we meet again. Drink Man. Girl, you keep this up and I'm gonna think you following me.

You're on the dance floor having a good time. You turn around.

Jackass: Remember me? Drink Man. Yeah, come on, girl, I paid for that drink. You owe me.

Me: Look, you better get the hell away from me. You gave me a drink, not a kidney.

Skeet Skeet

I've been in quite a few strip clubs. Hey, I'm a comic on the road working with a bunch of men. It's pretty much a given that I'm ending up in a strip club during my travels. Florida by far has more strip clubs than any other state I've been through. Florida got so many strip clubs, they need to change their state flag to just a brass pole. "Florida, the ass-showing state."

I went to this one strip club, and they actually tried to charge me a cover. Can you believe that? Wanted me to pay. I was like, "Pay? Are you out your damn mind?" I was like, "Come on, man. I brought my own titties. You really don't expect me to pay to see titties. I can see titties for free all day if I want to. Hell, I can even play with them. Can you do that in there? I didn't think so. Come on, BYOT, man."

I'm not gonna lie to y'all. Once I got inside and saw those triple-Gs and stuff, I went back and paid. I was like, "Oh, oh. I get it now. I see. Those are professional titties in there. My titties couldn't do that." I guess if your titties are bigger than your head, then yeah. You should be able to pay some bills with them.

Go check out the strip clubs, ladies. I promise you, lots of laughs. Did you know that they actually put ATM machines in the strip clubs? Did you know that? I think it's unfair.

They are just taking advantage of the poor horny bastards. There should be some zoning law where these guys should not be able to have access to their money in the same room with naked women. Naked ass in the same area of an ATM machine spells overdrawn for these guys. You should see them, too. Just running to the ATM machine, the stripper is punching in his PIN code with her nipple. He's just happy. "I think she likes me." I'm like, "Get your dumb ass away from the machine."

I went to this one club in Florida. Man, that was the end of strip clubs for me. It was like the lowest, the nastiest, I mean, just raw, naked ass. I got a glimpse of what Sodom and Gomorrah must have been like. It was so gross. There's no DJ, no liquor license. And the girls, they didn't even bother dancing. They just stood up there, legs spread wide open. "Look at it! Is that what you want, huh? Look at it!" I was like, "Oh, my God. I gotta get up outta here."

But the guys, they were just in there looking at it. And it's not like they were weird-lookin', freaky guys. They were just your regular, average-looking guys. But they just needed to look at it.

That's when I had a whole new respect for men. It must be really hard being a man. You guys have that thing up in your head, messing with you all the time. How do you get any work done? How do you guys hold down jobs, man? You know, you at work, minding your business, and all of a sudden that thing just kicks in. "Let's go look at it. Come on, man. When's the last time we seen it? Let's go look at it. Go to the ATM machine."

I was hoping to see some celebrities when I was hanging in the strip clubs. You gotta go to Atlanta to catch celebrities, especially athletes. At one time a club in Atlanta was under investigation for drugs and prostitution. They were questioning a lot of professional players. They said that Patrick Ewing and other pro players were in the strip club getting blow jobs and other sexual favors.

I don't think blowing Patrick Ewing should be considered a sexual favor. That is more like a sexual sacrifice. Patrick looks like Early Man; he probably has a prehistoric dick. It probably has a knot on it. And you thought his knees were bad!

Vegas

I love Vegas. No wait, I love casinos. That's the one place they don't allow kids. You can see kids running around Vegas, but they don't allow their little asses on the casino floor. If I could get a room with a king bed between the roulette wheel and the blackjack table, then that would be the perfect getaway. On the casino floor there's just grown people drinking and throwing their money away. I never go to Vegas expecting to win money. I always go with a limit of how much I'm going to lose, including clothes and self-respect.

I almost got kicked out the last time I was in Vegas. I know you're thinking, What in the world did her crazy ass do to get kicked out of Vegas? It was some bullshit. First of all, like any other story about getting kicked out or getting shot, they all start with, "Okay, I had been drinking, maybe I was a little drunk." Yep, that was my condition. When I'm drunk, that's when I feel a lucky streak coming on. There's no strategy behind gambling, so I like to do it when I'm drunk to remove all reasoning and thought. I'm the one yelling, "Hit me" at the blackjack table when I have eighteen. Hey, they don't call the game Twenty-one for nothing. I want twenty-one, dammit.

Of course I was losing, so I was cursing. "Thirty, aww,

fuck, busted again." After a few hands, the pit boss comes over and says, "You can't use that type of language here." I'm like, "What language? This is Vegas and it's three o'clock in the morning." I can't think of anything that I could possibly say that would be a problem in Vegas. Seriously, I can't. Maybe, "I have a bomb." But then again, have you seen some of the high rollers? I think even if you say some shit like that, if you haven't gone over your limit, they'll still let you play. So I ask the pit boss, "What the fuck are you talking about?" And he says, "You said the F word." I thought he was fucking with me, so I said, "Man, quit fucking with me." He got pissed. He was serious. "If you continue to use that language, I will have security remove you from the casino." Now I'm thinking this is some bullshit. "This is Vegas, anything goes! I can pay somebody to fuck me, but you're saying I can't say 'fuck'? Man, fuck you!" So now he gets on the phone to security and the three black men who I was with scatter like roaches when you turn on the light.

Everybody runs except for my friend Dino. Dino don't give a fuck. Dino stayed right there, trying to get me to run, too. "Come on, Wanda, let's get the fuck up outta here. This is your favorite casino, you don't want to get kicked out of this mu'fucka." I was so touched by my good friend Dino looking out for me that I turned to the pit boss and said, "Dino said 'fuck,' call security on him, too." That's when Dino turned to another friend who was hiding behind the slot machines and gave up his wallet, jewelry, and coat. Dino was like, "Wanda, you might joke your way out of this, but my black ass is going to jail." I wasn't going to let that happen.

After ten minutes passed, no security, no nothing. So I mosey over to the pit boss and say, "Hey, man, where the fuck is security?" He gets irate. He's like, "That's it. You're outta here." So he picks up the phone. I didn't move. When you're in the right, don't budge. I didn't do shit, so I wasn't going to run. This conservative asshole was trying to impose some personal standard that he had set as proper behavior for women. So what, he picks up the phone? I didn't care. I'm thinking, Unless he's calling my mother, I ain't scared. As long as I don't hear, "Is she out there showing her ass again?" I'm not moving.

Eventually security shows up; yeah, I waited for them. These big dudes walk up to me smiling, like they were surprised that I was still there. I didn't even let them ask me what was going on. I said, "Man, this muthafucka is trippin' because I said 'fuck.'" They laughed their asses off. Then they told me to take my drunk ass to bed. Dino stopped praying and we all went home. I love Vegas. That pit boss probably saved me a couple of hundred dollars.

Smoke Up

When President Reagan was in office, he said that marijuana was *the* most dangerous drug and threat to America. It causes memory loss . . . naw, too easy. Why was it the most dangerous threat? Because America wasn't making any money off of it. Once you've had some Colombian, domestic just doesn't cut it anymore.

Like my man Jimmy Carter, I'm for decriminalizing marijuana. As long as tobacco is legal, marijuana should be legal, too. I'd rather be in a room full of weed smoke than cigarette smoke. With weed smoke I'm looking for a bag of chips, not for a lump in my breast.

At least weed has medicinal uses. It clears up glaucoma, helps AIDS and cancer patients get an appetite, and it gives relief to chronic pain sufferers. No doctor has ever told a patient, "Smoke a half a pack of Newports, that should help clear that up."

Pain, who's to say who can cope with pain? We all have different thresholds. If I get a headache, why can't I smoke a joint? Advil upsets my stomach. I'm a chronic sinus sufferer. I get a sinus infection as often as Bobby Brown goes to jail. Why can't I tell my ENT, "Doc, that antibiotic you gave me is not doing the job. I think I need a dime bag of hydro. The poor air quality doesn't bother me when I'm high."

I get so angry when on the news they show DEA agents out in a field with flame shooters, destroying a perfectly good crop of marijuana. I'm like, "What the hell? They are setting it on fire. We were going to do the same thing. It may have taken me a little longer to get rid of all of it, but basically we're on the same team, man. What's the difference? Just because you have on a jacket with some letters on the back of it makes it okay for you to light it up? What if I wore my old high school letterman jacket while I smoke? Is that okay?"

It's ridiculous watching them destroy something that naturally grows out of the ground. Why? Just because our government says it's illegal. The government says they're looking out for our safety. They are trying to protect the public. Well, I hate lilies. The big ones, they stink and make me sneeze. I want to see some DEA agents out there setting a greenhouse of lilies on fire. If anybody is caught buying or selling them, throw their lily-loving ass in jail. These people are useless. All they want to do is sit around and smell their lilies all day. Lock 'em up!

I'm sick of the government lying to us about how they are trying to protect the public. That's bullshit. The government is trying to protect their pockets. The government doesn't give a damn about our health. They say they don't know enough about marijuana and the mental effects. So? They know everything about alcohol. People die every day from alcohol. Alcohol and the effects of alcohol will kill you. And not only is it legal, you go out to a club and there's a two-drink minimum. How can our government, which claims it wants to protect us, allow establishments to make us drink? What a bunch of hypocrisy. If you need a liver transplant, don't come see me at the comedy club, because they're gonna make you drink.

Now don't get me wrong. I'm not saying that alcohol should be illegal. Lord knows, I wouldn't want to live in a world where ya can't get a good margarita. I'm just saying that we should be able to enjoy a fat joint along with it. Stop "protecting" us, and dictating what drug we use to destroy ourselves. However, there should be zero tolerance for those freakin' lily-heads.

Actually, I don't smoke weed . . . that often, because I have things to do. Like most weed smokers, I don't get much done when I'm high. I giggle and point, that's about the most that I can handle. I have to schedule my weed. "Let's see. Tuesday is wide open. I don't have any meetings. Let's pencil this in, Weed Day. Tuesday is now Weedsday."

Alcohol and the occasional weed is it for me. I haven't tried and don't plan on trying any other drug. I'm too scared . . . or for the kids, I'll say I'm too smart. I can be a loud asshole when I'm drunk, so I know me coked up? Somebody's gonna shoot me. Plus, I don't like the whole drug culture. I see somebody snortin' coke, I leave the room. It amazes me how they keep talking like they didn't do anything. That's scary. I need a noise or something. When you do a shot, you groan or do a "whoo-hoo, yeah!" When you take a hit off a joint you cough or say, "Yeah, that's good shit." But I've seen people snort coke and never miss a beat of conversation. I'm like, "Damn, acknowledge that you just had a rolled-up ten-dollar bill up your nose or something." Cocaine is all denial. Shit, even when you take a vitamin you say something like, "I feel a cold coming, trying to kick it with some vitamin C."

When you get past weed, that whole drug culture is shady. It becomes very dark. Your life is in danger. At least if you drink too much and get alcohol poisoning, somebody is gonna try to help you. They might kill you in a car crash on the way to the hospital, but they tried to help you. If you have a bad weed experience, somebody is gonna try to help you. You might die while they are trying to call 911. "Man, we gotta call nine-one-one. What's the number?" But some-body is gonna try to help you. You OD around some real drug addicts, that's your ass. Drug people get the fuck out and take your wallet with them. Nobody is trying to go to jail for your dead ass. You might as well get in the position of how you want your chalk outline portrait to be.

Man, as soon as I finish writing this book, I'm getting fucked up!

Part Twelve

Purple Pain

School is in and Prince is the teacher, baby. I love Prince. I stayed with him through the name changes and everything. I love that little sexy bastard. He's a genius. I'm so excited he's back. I have something to look forward to musically. When Prince opened the Grammys with Beyoncé, I was right there in front of my TV with the Tivo rollin'. That was just a preview to what was to come, because I had tickets to go see him live at the House of Blues later that night. I was downright giddy.

The show didn't start until a little after midnight, but that was cool with me. I was ready for some "dance, music, sex, romance." Prince was absolutely amazing, as usual. I've seen him live about seven or eight times. His band, the New Power Generation, was tight. Onstage there was all of these candles and drapes, it was sexy as hell. After two hours, Prince was still going strong, we were jammin' our ass off. Then it dawned on me that Prince needs to recognize that the bulk of his fans are over thirty. Some time after two in the morning I was checking out the crowd; everybody was leaning on something, the wall, the bar, the stage, a rail, each other. There were people holding their shoes and fanning themselves, women and men. Shit, we were tired, but we were having a ball.

After another hour passed, my friend Alyson was like, "If that purple mu'fucka plays one more song, I'm gonna go up onstage and blow those drippy-ass candles out myself." We were hurting. I'm ashamed to say that we started wishing evil shit on him because we are die-hard fans. I wasn't about to leave before the show was over. So we were like:

"Oh God, please break his boot heel."

"Take his voice, Lord."

"Shock him, Father, not enough to hurt him, just enough to make him stop."

"Earthquake." (It was California.)

"Fire, not one of those Great White fires, just some smoke to close the place down."

I think his Royal Badness finally caught on that we don't have it in us to party as long as he can and around 3:30, he finally said good night. That was probably the best night of my life.

Of course, on the way home, Alyson and I talked about how we would never fuck Prince, because he wouldn't know when to stop.

O

Oprah is like a god to us. We view her as someone we can pray to at night to make our lives better. She hands out blessings. She's always giving something away on her show, "my favorite things," the Angel Network, matching P. Diddy's marathon donation. I don't know what her ancestors told her, but mine told me to hang on to my shit. Giving away things we've worked for is what got us here in the first place. What kills me is that everybody has an opinion on how Oprah should spend her money. That's not fair. Can we just let her keep and enjoy her own money? We love Oprah so much we talk about her as though she were a member of our family.

"Guess what Oprah did the other day? She rented a private island for a weekend getaway for all her rich friends."

"She needs to invite people like us who never get to go anywhere or do anything. All we do is work, work, work. All she does is sit up there and talk for one hour a day. I do that on my porch every day and I don't get paid shit!"

The nerve of some people, please. We should allow Oprah to do what rich people do. Spend money on wasteful shit. I wanna see Oprah on BET's *How I'm Living*, driving up to her studio, flipping switches in a Bentley bouncing on hydraulics. Gail chillin' in the backseat, holding the remote, watching a DVD on the plasma-screen TV in the headrest. She deserves it! When I see Oprah smile, I wanna see a few diamonds imbedded in her platinum front teeth. She deserves it! Rather than building a library in Africa, I wanna see Oprah with a heavy-ass platinum chain around her neck. She's earned it! She should hook Stedman up with one, too. His and her chains. That's how I wanna see Oprah live.

Whitney and Bobby

I love Tivo. I cannot erase that Diane Sawyer–Whitney Houston interview. I just can't. I tried to record a show on PBS, but Tivo said there was not enough room. It gave me the option to delete the Whitney interview and I was like, "Nope. Can't do it." I just love that damn interview. That was genius. Diane Sawyer was like, "What about these accusations of your drug use? Spending two, three hundred thousand dollars on drugs?" Whitney said, "Show me the receipts, where are the receipts?" I was thinking, Whitney is high. What is she doing, denying that she uses drugs and she's high? This is some Richard Pryor shit right here. "Where's the receipts?" 'Cause drug dealers are so meticulous with their taxes. "Let me see, that's four rocks, gotta add the eight-point-five-percent sales tax, and here is your receipt." I bet he had a punch card, too. Buy ten rocks, get one free.

The beauty is that when you look at Whitney and Bobby, you go, "Okay they live in a mansion." When family or girlfriends come over, you know they don't put their purse down. You know when you walk into your girlfriend's house you can just throw your purse on the couch. Well, when you walk into their mansion, first you ask, "Is Bobby home?"

"Yes."

"I'll hold on to my purse."

BB

I bet you Bobbi Brown the cosmetics guru is pissed she has the same name as Bobby Brown the crackhead. I've tuned in to *Oprah* several times thinking I was gonna see Oprah get Bobby off the pipe, but it was Bobbi getting women off of blue eye shadow. I met her at a Nets play-off game, very nice lady. But when they told me Bobbi Brown wanted to meet me, I was like, "Aw, shit, Bobby Brown is here? Where's my purse?" So you know Bobbi Brown is like, "Damn, I've worked hard all my life for people to mistake me for a crackhead?"

What if Bobby Brown the crackhead capitalized on his name and came out with his own line of makeup? "When you get your ass kicked by drug dealers you owe, you're gonna need lots of concealer. What can you do about all that sweat? Bobby Brown's powder and foundation. You can also try our natural lipstick for cracked-up lips."

Siegfried and Roy

I've never seen the Siegfried and Roy show, but if they ever make it back to the stage, I will be there in the front row wearing a poncho like I was at a Gallagher concert. I don't blame the tiger for snapping at all. They said that the tiger attacked because he became disoriented. Well, yeah, he's in a damn casino! A tiger does not belong in a casino. I love Vegas and I love to gamble, but after five hours in a casino I'm ready to rip somebody's throat out.

Then they tried to blame the tiger snapping because of some woman's hair in the audience. Have you seen Siegfried's hair? The tiger works with Siegfried every day and they want to blame some woman from New Jersey for having big hair. I heard next time they have a show they'll have a sign that says your hair must be this tall in order for you to see this show.

As you can tell, I have little sympathy for people who get trampled running with the bulls, or crushed by an elephant at the circus, or any silly shit that involves a wild animal. Animals don't want to be in the damn circus, jumping through hoops on fire or standing on one foot. If they weren't so drugged up, more of them would snap. I mean, we have people doing regular jobs that lose it and shoot up their place of employment. I bet the post office would have way more casualties if we made them balance the mail on their noses.

Part Thirteen

Leave a Message
After the . . . *Click!*

I hate answering machines and voicemail. It just pisses me off. As soon as I hear that mechanical tone before a voice . . . *click!* I bail. I'm one of those people who won't leave anything but a dial tone as a message. Oh, you might catch a swear or two before I hang up, but that's it. I used to leave messages, but years of experience have taught me that the majority of outgoing messages are stupid. The only thing people need to say is, "Leave a message." That's all the information I need. Unfortunately, people tend to feel that an outgoing message gives them a license to be creative. Stop irritating people and go buy a clay wheel. Let me give you a few examples of the kind of outgoing messages that have made me wish we still communicated by drums.

If I call to ask you what time the movie starts, I don't want to be serenaded. Just because you broke up with your boyfriend, why do I have to listen to Beyoncé? "Me, myself, and I. That's all I've got in the end. I'ma be my own best friend . . . I can't come to the phone right now, but I'm strong. Leave a message after the tone and I'll get back to you." *Beep!*

I lose it. "Look, I just called to tell you, yourself, and that other bitch that I can't make it to the show. I decided to stay in and rent a movie with your ex. We're going to get high and watch *Fatal Attraction*. Girl, you didn't tell me you branded his initials on your back. No wonder he left your crazy ass. And don't bother calling me back tonight. I'll be screening."

Other people I hate are the ones who think it's cute to help their kids record their message. That would only be amusing if the kid was retarded. Let me give you an example. Now bear with me. This is a book, so you've really got to imagine a really retarded kid saying these things.

"Say, we can't come to the phone right now."

"Eight."

"But leave a message after the beep . . ."

"Graham cracker feet."

"And we'll get back to you as soon as possible."

"No more hospitals." *Beep!*

"Haaaaa! I know I've called you at least ten times, but that shit is hilarious. I'm going to hang up and call you right back. I want to let my nephew hear it. We laughed our ass off when I took him to see that movie *Radio*."

C'mon, retarded kids are funny. Besides, you're probably reading this book alone, so it's okay to laugh. Then again, if somebody's reading it to you, then you might be retarded. But if this bit just downright makes you uncomfortable, pretend the retarded kid is Frankenstein and read it again. It's still funny.

Now the best argument I can think of against stupid outgoing messages has to be 9/11. You would think that would have taught people a lesson. Can you imagine how a person on one of those flights would have felt if they'd have wasted their last phone call on one of these?

"Hello? It's me. I don't have a lot of time. The plane's been hijacked and we're all going to die. I just wanted to tell you that I love you and—"

"Gotcha! Ha ha, I'm not home right now, but leave a message after the tone and I'll call you back." *Beep!*

"Fuck!" *Click!*

"Let's roll."

"What?!"

Leave a Message

When you call me, do me a favor. Leave me messages saying why you called. Do not leave a message telling me to call you, because I won't. "Hey, Wanda, it's Dino. Call me." Why? I sense no urgency in your message. At least mention jail, or bail, or drinks or something. Don't be all vague or you will not hear from me. I figure if you're just calling to talk, you'll call back.

The only person I call immediately back is my gynecologist. In fact, she can be in the process of leaving a message for me and she'll have to click over to pick up my incoming call back to her. "Yeah, Doc, you were calling me, what's up? Everything okay?" Other than her, you'd better leave me some info.

Hey, That's Me!

I want a clone. That would be so cool. Somebody to hang with when I didn't feel like being bothered with anybody but myself. Somebody that I could relate to, who'd always love me no matter what. Like a sister, but without the sibling rivalry or jealousy. Boy, we'd get along great, Cloney and me. That's what I'd name her, Cloney. What a great alibi she'd make. Or a witness. "Your Honor, that wasn't me driving that truck. I was miles away, at home. Alone. Ask Cloney." Some say that clone research is a sin. But where's the sin in having your very own "occasional" decoy if necessary? For protection. The Lord helps those who help themselves. I'd be helping myself two times over. If a crazed fan started stalking me, I could just send Cloney out like bait. Then I could shop without being bothered. I wouldn't even tell anybody I had a clone. We could trick people just like in *Freaky Friday*. Or rob banks, just like in *Heat*. I could literally be in two places at once. Plus, if something ever went wrong with me physically, like say with my kidneys or heart or liver, I'd have all those parts available. Sure, some people think mankind would commit great sins by only using our clones to harvest new body parts. Well, to that I have two rebuttal comments. Number One: "Not me, Cloney and I would be great pals." And Number Two: "And?" A clone would be like an organ savings account. If my liver was overdrawn, I'd just deposit another one from my account. What's going on with clone research and development? I'm ready for mine.

My Beneficial Mouth

I always get in trouble when people tell me what not to say.
I'm like a kid with a hot stove. One show, I did a benefit for a
feminist organization. Benefit means no money. So I figure I
should be able to say what I want to say. I figured if I pissed
them off, who cares? What are they going to do? Get mad
and pay me? There is nothing to lose. So it's all feminists.
Gloria Steinem was sitting right up front. I walked out and
said, "Look here, I can't stay around here too long with you
broads because I gotta get home and cook my man a nice hot
dinner. Plus, he likes a blow job by nine forty-five." I thought
it was funny. They didn't. They didn't find anything funny. I
thought, Oh Lord, I made these women mad. I stepped over
the line. I continued. "Ladies, calm down. I'm just joking. He
likes a blow job anytime."

Fans

I quickly learned that being on TV is a lot of responsibility. If it sucks, people will tell you, "Oh, you suck." And there are people who are not afraid to tell you. People come up to me on the street, "You look so good in person. Girl, that camera don't love you." I don't understand the logic behind doing something like that in the first place. You don't tell the person you recognize in a police lineup that they suck. You don't even want them to know you exist. You're too scared to see how they'll react. I wish they'd treat seeing people on TV the same way. We're both behind a glass; we can't see who's watching us. Well, that's what I would prefer these people to do. Act like I'm one of those crazed-looking psychopath girls who's been interrupted. Don't know what I'm gonna do or say next. No telling what medication they got me on that day.

Fans think they can come up and say anything to me. It's cool because they feel like I'm accessible, down to earth, and approachable. I am all those things, when you got something nice to say. But you can keep that negative shit to yourself. "I thought you looked way fatter on TV."

I really don't give a damn what a fan thinks about my personal appearance. Do fans actually think I look in the mirror and ask myself, Hmmm. I wonder what the fans will think of my outfit tonight? Maybe I should put on the bright red lipstick for the fans. They'd really appreciate it.

I was picking up some takeout and the guy in the kitchen yelled, "Wanda, you cut your hair. I liked it better longer." Oh my bad, next time I'll come down here to the chicken joint and ask your greasy ass for permission.

The fans never cross my mind when I'm getting my hair done. Now when I'm in a Motel 6 shooting heroin with three strippers, that's when I think, How will the fans feel? I'm joking. I'd never stay at a Motel 6.

But seriously, if you see me on the street, don't come up to me. I am off work. That means I am not working. That means I am not performing at the current time, please redirect your route. Thank you. I mean, it's one thing to just say hello, but people will come up to me and say, "Say something funny." "Fuck you." Then they laugh. As I walk away I think, That's not a joke. Fuck you. Like I'm a damn toy. Look into its eyes and it'll make you laugh.

One time I was just standing at the corner waiting for the light, minding my own business, and this old lady came up to me and pinched my titty. After molesting me, she laughed and said, "Girl, you crazy." I'm crazy? Who's the one going around pinching titties? You're the crazy one. See how y'all treat me? I bet you no one ever walked up and grabbed Maya Angelou's titty.

Bad Show Ideas

The whole process of getting a decent idea to work requires a walk through hell for a warmup. See, before you get to do a show that you want to do, you gotta listen to all of their bad ideas. And they have a lot of bad ideas. After hearing them from my representation, I'd think, Do people actually say yes to these roles? and Why am I paying you? Aren't you supposed to filter this bullshit out before it gets to me? I would hear shit that would really fuck with my mind. It made me forget what year it was. My agent would call me, and she's like:

Agent: Wanda, they want you to play a maid. . . . And you win the lottery. But you love working for this family so much that you continue to be their maid.

Me: Set it up. I want to meet these people. So I can slap the shit out of them.

The Millionaire Maid. What the hell is that? I think, What am I doin'? Cleaning the toilets with my thousand-dollar bills? "How you doin', Senator? Oh, I love this maidin'." What the hell is that? What makes you think people want to work for you like that? That's ridiculous. I'm gonna tell you right now, if somebody walked in here and told me I just won the lottery, I would stop writing in the middle of this book. The rest would be a journal of blank pages for you to fill in. I love to make people laugh and everything, but I'd love to sit on my ass all day and watch *Real World* marathons.

What's next? I play a single mother with twelve children. All fathered by different men. Call it *Who's Your Daddy?* You know, it'd be like one of those reality shows. I'd travel the country with a DNA expert. Voting daddies off. Last daddy standing owes a million dollars in child support.

I would hear shit where my body wouldn't even allow me to go through the motions, just for money. Although I've turned down gigs and imagined a single woman glaring at me, with four jobs and five kids, struggling, screaming, "Who the fuck are you? You got some nerve!"

Turning down money like that makes you feel a little arrogant. Some of y'all are going, "No, it makes *you* feel arrogant; it would make me feel stupid." I hear ya, but I know if I did some sellout bullshit y'all would be the first ones to say, "Damn, what's up with Wanda? You see that bullshit? She fell off, man. She sold out."

If you sell out, you gotta do it big. You gotta do the things that pay big. Roles where you have at least one hand on your hip the whole movie, or white people hit you with food, or my favorite, the dance number.

Expectations

I apologize to those of you who are reading this book with complete disappointment. I know some readers out there are expecting me to say certain things. Now I'll admit and say, "Yeah, I said it" when I say some off-the-wall crazy shit. But there are a few things that I refuse to let come out my mouth. It's not just common folk who have these expectations; it's people in the industry, as well. If a writer, director, or producer ever suggests that I say any of these lines, I simply reply, "Naw, I ain't saying that bullshit." I guarantee that you will never hear me say any of the following sayings:

1. I'm gonna shove my foot up yo' ass.
2. Oh, no she didn't.
3. Talk to the hand.
4. You better recognize.
5. You better bring it.
6. Check yourself before you wreck yourself.
7. You go, girl.
8. Don't go there.
9. You can't touch this.
10. I'm about to knock this fool out.
11. I'ma smack the taste right outta your mouth.

12. Fo' sheezy, my neezy.

13. Poof. Be gone. You do not exist.

And you'll never see me do the following:

1. The Karate Kid stance.

2. Soul Plane 2.

3. Raise the roof.

4. Electric slide at the Emmys . . . again.

5. The chicken dance anywhere.

After reading this list, if you find yourself disheartened, kiss my ass.

Me and the Beast

When I was going around whoring myself for *Wanda at Large,* I did *Jimmy Kimmel Live.* I was selling that sweet ass. The guest host was Mike Tyson. Oh my God, I've never been so scared before in my life. I know I talk a lot of shit, but I'm gonna tell ya, that night I was like a deaf mute. When I did the preinterview, the one important thing Kimmel's people failed to mention to me was that Mike Tyson was going to be on the show. He was cohosting all week long and they didn't tell me. Talkin' about "we forgot." How the hell do you forget Mike Tyson is in the building? I remember stuff about Mike way back in 1989. How do you forget that?

I get to the *Jimmy Kimmel Live* studio and I'm walking up to the studio doors and I'm looking around like, "Man, there's an awful lot of security guards out here. What the hell's going on out here?" Just big-ass dudes. That Jimmy Kimmel must be pretty wild. There was a guy with a pith helmet and a tranquilizer gun standing in the corner. I thought to myself, Maybe Jack Hanna is on the show. I like zoo animals. Maybe there are some exotic animals on the show. So I think I'm gonna be petting a koala bear or something and crazy-ass Mike Tyson is out there. In his chair, salivating, just waiting for that right moment to take a chunk out of my ass.

If you saw the show, you noticed that I didn't sit down. I went out there and Jimmy Kimmel is sitting at his desk, or as I referred to it, a potential protective shield. Mike Tyson was sitting right next to me with no type of barrier, obstacle, or weapon between us. So I had to make sure I didn't sit down all the way. It was just like I had one cheek on the edge of the chair. So if something breaks out, I'm heading for the nearest emergency exit. I was like an Olympic sprinter. I was in the blocks. I was looking at Jimmy like, "Okay, as soon as this mutherfucker snaps, just give me the sign. And I am outta here." I felt like that lady from the *When Animals Attack* video. Remember when that bear jumped that woman? That's what I felt like, any minute this man is gonna maul me to death. I was thinking, Lord, please get me outta here with my panties on. If I can keep my panties, I will praise Your name. If I can just hold on to my drawers, it'll be all good. And I didn't want to look at him because Mike got that crazy-ass tattoo on his face. He looks like a Borg from *Star Trek*. "You will be assimilated. Resistance is futile." Then he started talking to me. I was trying not to look at him because I didn't want to rile him up. Plus, you can't look a bear straight in the eye. Then Mike just broke out singing: "Wanda Sykes, Wanda Sykes." I was like, "Aw, shit. Jimmy, you better wrap this up quick." Then he said something crazy, "I like your socks." "I'm not wearing any socks, Mike, but thank you." I'm thinking, Did I hear the starting gun? Because I'm about to take off.

During the commercial break he asked me one chilling question: "So what type of guys do you like?" I thought, Oh Lord, there go the panties. I'm done for, that's it. Maybe if I can just hold on to my panty band everything will be okay. Now when Mike Tyson asks you that question, you can't say the response you wanna say, which is, "Not you." You can't say that because it's Mike Tyson. So I was like, "Uh . . . type of guys? Albino midgets. Aw, Mike, I love me some albino midgets. Woooo, I tear that ass up! Aw, Mike, they're like turkey meat. I love me some albino midgets. Can't get enough of them. You know any?"

So at the end of the show I'm getting excited, thinking I

survived. I thought I was home free. I had to go backstage to grab my belongings and make a fast getaway, but in order to do so I had to pass his dressing room. So I'm walking past his dressing room, trying to sneak by, and I look and he's sitting in there with a big pile of weed getting fucked up! So I started thinking . . . You know . . . Mike ain't so bad. He's not that scary. He's just misunderstood. You got to get to know someone before you can judge him like that. Next thing you know, I'm passing the blunt to Mike. "So, Mike, you like my socks?" "Yeah." "Cool, man."

Now Mike, if you just read that story, remember, I'm a comic. I make people laugh for a living. I make up funny stories. I sincerely had an enjoyable time with you. I think you are a very nice man. Please don't punch me in the face. If I disrespected you, remember, I'm a comic. I tell funny stories. Please don't punch me in the face. If you wanna punch somebody, punch Jimmy Kimmel in the face for having a show. If he didn't have a show, you would not have been there. I would not have been there. This story would have never been told. Besides, Jimmy has enough shows, *The Man Show, Crank Yankers*. What the hell is he doing with another show, trying to cause some beef between you and me? Or punch my agent in the face for getting me this book deal. If he didn't get me this deal, I never would have written that shit. Or better yet, punch my publisher in the face. If they hadn't offered me this deal, this muthafucka would have never been printed. So there!

About the Author

WANDA SYKES is a favorite recurring guest on HBO's Emmy Award–winning series *Curb Your Enthusiasm*, and lends her distinctive comedic perspective to HBO's *Inside the NFL* as a field correspondent. She earned an Emmy for Outstanding Writing for a Variety, Music, or Comedy Special for *The Chris Rock Show*. Wanda starred in her own Fox TV sitcom in 2003, *Wanda at Large*, and performed her own television comedy special, *Tongue Untied*. In 1999 she received the American Comedy Award for Outstanding Funniest Female Stand-Up Comic. Born in Portsmouth, Virginia, and raised in Maryland, Sykes lives in Los Angeles.